You Can Make It Happen

A Guide To Self-Actualization and Organizational Change

You Can Make It Happen

A Guide To Self-Actualization and Organizational Change

LEN SPERRY
U.S. International University, San Diego
DOUGLAS J. MICKELSON
University of Wisconsin, Milwaukee
PHILLIP L. HUNSAKER
University of Wisconsin, Milwaukee

ADDISON-WESLEY PUBLISHING COMPANY
Reading, Massachusetts • Menlo Park, California
London • Amsterdam • Don Mills, Ontario • Sydney

Copyright © 1977 by Len Sperry. Philippines copyright 1977 by Len Sperry.
All rights reserved. No part of this publication may be reproduced, stored in a retrieval system, or transmitted, in any form or by any means, electronic, mechanical, photocopying, recording, or otherwise, without the prior written permission of the publisher. Printed in the United States of America. Published simultaneously in Canada. Library of Congress Catalog Card No. 76-45156.

ISBN 0-201-07129-0
ABCDEFGHIJ-DO-7987

For those who mean so much to us:
Tracy, Sue, Chris, Mike;
Annette, Hans, Christopher, Alexander;
Jo, Phillip, Kathy, Sarah.

Preface

Almost all people are members of organizations, be they job, social, or family. They may be nurses on hospital medical teams, supervisors in business or industry, graduate students trying to complete degree requirement, executives attempting to increase production, mothers attempting to raise children, etc. The organization in each instance can either help or hinder an individual in achieving his or her immediate as well as long-range goals for finding fulfillment in life, sometime called self-actualization. Organizations can provide the basis for "meeting one's needs" and for satisfaction *or* they can serve as a constant irritant and an avenue of dissatisfaction. One might wonder why it is that some people really seem to enjoy their jobs, while others, who are equally as bright and talented, are unhappy and discontented working at the same jobs. The reasons for this conflict are many, as author/interviewer Studs Terkel (1974) points out in his provocative best seller, *Working.*

But the basic reason for satisfaction or dissatisfaction seems to be the level of *match* between a person's needs and level of personal and professional development and the needs and demands of the organization, as well as the organization's level of social and ideological development. The thesis of this book is quite simply, "The better the match between person and organization, the greater the chances for satisfaction and self-actualization; the greater the mismatch, the greater the chances for dissatisfaction and self-stagnation."

Self-help books on the subject of self-actualization have abounded in the past few years. Yet, in many of these books, self-fulfillment is viewed strictly from an individualistic stance, and self-actualization is described in terms of personal decisions, feelings, and achievements. In most of these books, the role of organization imposes on the individual, organizational dimension, and internal and external demands on the individual (all of which in many cases militate against satisfaction and fulfillment) are neglected. Often the assumption is that the organization should be viewed as an "enemy to be avoided" because its reward and support systems seem to favor "adjusted," "don't-rock-the-boat," and "don't-grow" behavior. In other words, self-actualization and organizational behavior are viewed as antithetical.

Today, nearly everyone in an organization who is responsible for making decisions, at even the lowest levels of the organization, has the potential for being a *change agent*. A doctoral degree or O.D. experience is not needed. Personnel managers, systems analysts, production people, nurses, teachers, or case workers in community mental health centers can and have learned the assessment and intervention techniques necessary for changing their organizations. In addition to learning the skills of change agentry, these individuals need to learn that a change in an organization often requires a corresponding change or growth in the change agents themselves. Flexibility and nondefensiveness seem to be prerequisite attitudes that the prospective change agent must learn along with change tactics.

We believe that the informed person can learn to make assessments of self and his or her needs, aspirations, and level of psychological development as well as of the organization and its level of development. This individual can then make intelligent decisions about whether to "adjust" to work demands, "change" the environment, "leave" the job, or "change" self. This book offers a blueprint for such analyses and serves as a basis for planning a program of action, whether it be personal change, organizational change, or both. Such an understanding of how people and organizations "match up" serves as the basis for a plan of action for the projected change. A series of strategies for planning, complementing, and evaluating the proposed change are included. Case material illustrates the procedure and process.

It is our desire that this book will provide hope and encouragement to those individuals who feel trapped in their organization. We also hope that this book will stimulate a new breed of change agents who will go forth and help to humanize their organizations and themselves at the same time.

January 1977   **L.S.**
                                                                                        D.J.M.
                                                                                        P.L.H.

Contents

1 **You, Your Organization, and Change**   1

   Four case studies 1
   The person and his or her need for growth in
   organizations 6
   Opportunities for self-actualization within organizations   8
   Barriers to self-actualization in organizations 9
   Overcoming barriers to self-actualization: Being your
   own change agent 11
   A word about self-actualization 12

2 **How Individuals Develop and Change**   15

   Stages of adult development 17
   Values and behavior 25
   Development of a personality style 30
   Putting it all together 35

3 **How Organizations Grow and Develop**   39

   Forces on the organization to grow and develop 40
   Forces on the organization to resist growth and
   development 43
   Stages of organizational growth and development 45
   Organizational climate 50

Effects of climate and structure on organizational members 55

4 The Personal Development Strategy: A Systematic Process for Personal and Organizational Development — 63

Change vs. planned change vs. personalized change 64
Why a personal development strategy? 65
A description of the personal development strategy 66
Self-actualization as a goal and criterion for personalized change 71
Criticisms of self-actualization as a criterion for change 73
How we define self-actualization 75
A concluding note 76

5 Finding Out Where You're At — 77

Where to begin—awareness 79
How to assess yourself 84
Developmental stage assessment exercise 84
Developmental stage assessment questionnaire 85
What the developmental stage assessment can tell you 88
Identifying our needs and values 88
What the value clarification process can tell you 94
Assessing your personality style 95
Your personal value index 98
The case of Ron and Janet Samuels 98

6 Understanding Your Organization — 101

How to assess your organization 103
Organizational assessment exercise 103
Organizational assessment questionnaire 103
Scoring the organizational assessment exercise 105
What the organizational assessment can tell you 106
The case of Joe Brennon 109

7 Making a Decision — 111

Your four options 111

A decision-making grid	113
The match-mismatch index	117
The person-organization decision-making grid	121

8 Implementing and Evaluating Your Development Program — 127

Self-actualization as a criterion	128
"One man's meat is another man's poison"	129
Performance criteria and "best fit"	129
Steps for implementation-evaluation	131
The case of Dick Larson resolved	135

9 Strategies for Self-Change — 139

Surviving	140
Letting go	141
Deciding to change	142
Tips for being successful in self-change	144
Selecting your self-change strategy	147
Physical conditioning	149
Desensitization/relaxation	150
Sensitivity training	153
Assertiveness training	154
Psychotherapy	156
Modeling	156
Role-playing	157
Bibliotherapy	158
Rational behavior training	159
Thought stopping	160
Implementing your self-change strategy—the case of Ron and Janet Samuels	161
Specific goals for change	165
Operationalizing the goal	166
Establishing subgoals	167
Building in rewards	167
Check points	167

10 Strategies for Organizational Change — 169

Role of an inside change agent — 170
Considerations in choosing a change strategy — 183
Interpersonal strategies for organizational change — 185
Organizational change strategies for more experienced facilitators — 192
Guide to selection of organizational change strategies — 197
References to organizational change strategies — 198
Implementing Joe Brennon's change plan — 199

11 Concluding Notes — 205

References — 206

Index — 209

Chapter 1

You, Your Organization, and Change

Every day we observe people who are unhappy, dissatisfied, or distressed. The source of these negative feelings often involves a person's job or role in an organization. And any way we look at it, we are all members of organizations—be they job, family, civic, or social. Being a member of an organization is a necessary element for most of us. Deep down most of us agree that "we are not islands," that we need structures and the other people in organizations to confirm our belief that we are worthwhile, useful people. But we also know that structures and people can cause us anguish. Four case studies follow.

FOUR CASE STUDIES

Dick Larson

Dick Larson, age 39, had been with Lakeside Laboratories for two years when he developed the electron pacifier. What happened after that seemed miraculous. A separate project was set up with Dick named as project manager, which gave him a great sense of pleasure. According to his supervisor, James Halberson, the "sky was the limit" for Dick's future prospects with Lakeside.

After a very rewarding year with the project, Mr. Halberson and Dick decided that the R & D team needed someone to serve as liaison with the electronics division. Consequently, Wilfred Steggart was assigned to the R & D team.

Although Wilfred (or Fred as he liked to be called) was a genius who provided the team with brilliant assistance, after six months it became apparent, at least to Dick, that Fred was also a disruptive force. Fred thought nothing of calling Dick at home at 2:30 A.M. to discuss some "brainstorm" that had just occurred to him. It was becoming clear to Dick that Fred thought nothing of indiscriminately panning the project, its direction, and the people in it. Fred let everyone know how much time and energy *he* put into the project and made others feel guilty if they did not match his enthusiasm or overtime. It was not long before Dick felt that he was losing control of the project, his self-respect, and the satisfaction and commitment the job held for him.

Whenever Fred was mentioned in conversations with Dick's boss, Dick commented only on Fred's ability and positive contributions to the team's work. He never mentioned his own discomfort because he felt it would reveal weaknesses in himself and also because it was clear that Mr. Halberson was considerably impressed with Fred's work.

It was not long before Dick started looking for another job. After a few weeks he found an equivalent project-head position at a new laboratory in a nearby community. Dick accepted the position and started work immediately. He notified Mr. Halberson of his decision by letter, stating that he felt sure Fred could supply team leadership and that his decision to leave was due to health problems in his family.

James Halberson was considerably disturbed by this unusual resignation, especially since he had decided to place Fred in charge of another project. He had been thinking about how to explain this to Dick, in view of the obvious assistance Dick had acknowledged receiving from Steggart. Halberson had already been reviewing the resumes of individuals with backgrounds similar to Fred's.

When asked whether he wished to manage the electron pacifier group or the new project, Fred chose to manage the new project and a temporary project leader was assigned to the electron pacifier group. Mr. Halberson contacted Dick, asking him to reconsider his decision.

Jean Lawrence

Jean Lawrence, age 28, resigned as Market Research Manager of a very successful stereo-components manufacturer. She traded her $14,000 a year job with its associated status and challenge for a $600 a month job as an interior-design trainee with the largest firm in the city. To Jean, the potential satisfaction of being able to branch out on her own and channel her creative ideas was worth the year and a half or two years she would need to really learn the ins and outs of interior design that would eventually enable her to set up her own business.

After Jean received her BS in art history from a small private midwestern college, she found a position as Assistant to the Vice President of Marketing at SOK Electronics in the same city. Because of the tight job market at the time, Jean felt fortunate to have found any job at all. Although it paid a low salary and consisted of a variety of "Girl Friday" duties, it was a job.

Then, after a year spent completing a variety of small projects at SOK, Jean began to feel dissatisfied with the lack of responsibility and permanence that this "Jill-of-all-trades" position provided. However, the job market was still bleak and Jean liked her colleagues and the atmosphere at SOK. Consequently, one day she approached Mr. Pondy, the Vice President for whom she worked, and explained her situation. Because Jean's performance over the past year had been outstanding, Mr. Pondy helped Jean to analyze what projects and what it was about those projects that she really liked best. As a result, it was mutually decided that she would be given a permanent assignment as a market research analyst. Within a year Jean became the top market analyst at SOK. She enjoyed designing and analyzing the studies she conducted and her enthusiastic, optimistic attitude made her a favorite public-relations person with her clients. During her third year she was promoted to the position of Market Research Manager and became the first woman in SOK's history to hold a management position.

The public-relations and the project-design aspects of her job appealed to Jean and she derived some satisfaction from them. But she longed to be her own boss and to be able to use her artistic talents more directly in her work. For some time, she had been looking into careers in the applied-arts area. Interior decorating and design caught her attention, but in order for Jean to break into the interior-design field she would need either further study at an art school or to participate in an on-the-job training program. Fortunately for Jean, a large furniture company was starting a 12-month training program and Jean was chosen to participate in the program as one of three apprentices. After carefully assessing her financial and personal needs, Jean resigned her position as Market Research Manager to pursue her emerging interest in interior design and decorating.

Joe Brennon

Joe Brennon, age 32, was distressed. He was nervous and irritable. He suffered from frequent chest pains, tired easily, and experienced dizzy spells at the most inopportune times. A physical examination revealed no abnormalities and Joe's physician prescribed a mild sedative, assuring Joe that nothing was seriously wrong.

But Joe knew otherwise! He had recently been turned down for a promotion to associate professor at the university where he had been employed for the past three years. Although he still had two years remaining on his contract, the recent negative vote, along with his below-average merit increases, indicated to Joe that he did not "fit in." Joe had recently received an attractive offer from a well-known West Coast university. This offer was, in fact, the basis of Joe's dilemma.

Joe's wife had two years remaining in the nursing program she was enrolled in, and his two children were well established in the local school system. All were very happy with the community and the conditions in which they lived and did not wish to disrupt their personal lives. Consequently, a frequent fantasy that occurred to Joe was to somehow change the personal reaction of the university's department chairman and senior faculty members to one of acceptance of him as a competent colleague, instead of as one who unfortunately (according to them) did not "fit" the image of the business school professor because he wore shoulder length hair and a full beard.

Feeling overpowered by the organization and unable to change the need others in it had for a consistent conservative image, Joe experienced tremendous feelings of anxiety originating from his helplessness in the situation. Should he disrupt his family's happiness and his wife's career to free himself from the university? Although he hadn't expressed this course of action to his family yet, Joe felt that this was perhaps his only alternative—unless, by some miracle, the faculty and the chairman changed their perspective. Joe knew that he must make a decision soon, because he could not endure his physical discomfort and inefficiencies much longer and because his family was becoming very aware of his nervousness and irritability. Something had to be done soon if Joe was to avoid a personal and a family breakdown.

Ron Samuels

Ron and Janet Samuels have been married for eleven years. They have two children—Ron, Jr., ten, and Mary, seven. Ron was recently promoted from district manager to regional manager for a major tire manufacturer.

Ron and Janet, who were high school sweethearts, married when they were both 19. They started college after high school and one year later they were married. Their plan was for Ron to continue with college while Janet worked to support them. Janet did not like the idea of quitting school nor did she like the assembly line job she had to take, but they needed the money. Fortunately (or unfortunately) for Janet, she soon became pregnant and had to quit her job, which meant that Ron had to go to school nights and work days to support his family. After seven years, Ron received his degree. He then decided to continue night school until he received an MBA. Although Ron was away from his family almost every evening, he "made it up" to them on weekends.

Ron's hobbies and interests gradually changed over the years. Ron enjoyed reading a good book now and then and he became more and more interested in drama and the theater. But Janet's interests didn't change much. She enjoyed talking to her friends on the phone for long periods of time, and she had become a regular TV watcher. Although Ron felt that Janet was an excellent mother, he also felt that in the last two or three years their marital relationship had changed—even deteriorated. It seemed to him that they were growing apart. Ron felt that he was becoming a stranger in his own home. He had less and less in common with Janet and because he spent very little time with the children they seemed to act like "Janet's kids" when Ron was with them. Conversation between Ron and Janet was becoming more and more strained.

Ron suggested that they read some books together and discuss them. Janet tried but she couldn't really match Ron's enthusiasm or insight. Ron "thought" he still loved his wife but he found himself being quietly embarrassed when they socialized with Ron's business associates whose wives were college graduates and active in the arts and the community. Ron thought about a separation, counseling, or just living a life of quiet desperation, an alternative which left Ron numb.

Things couldn't be going better with his career, but his home situation was adversely affecting Ron. Compounding Ron's feelings of frustration and dissatisfacton were his guilt feelings. Ron felt that if he hadn't stopped Janet from finishing college things might have been different. What's he to do?

THE PERSON AND HIS OR HER
NEED FOR GROWTH IN ORGANIZATIONS

Basic to all four case studies is a disparity between individual and organizational needs. The primary reason for the dissatisfaction and change described in each case was a mismatch or "poor fit" between the individual's needs and the situation provided by the organization—whether at work or at home. Psychologists tell us that what makes us uniquely human is the fact that we can "choose" to better ourselves by developing our potentials. Human beings are the *only* creatures with this ability, and although they may not choose or be "allowed" to exercise this option, it is nevertheless there. Organizations can provide the basis for meeting individual needs and self-development *or* they can serve as a barrier and a source of constant dissatisfaction. If the latter situation prevails, the individual is faced with the task of either somehow changing it or remaining chronically dissatisfied.

Our approach rests on the belief that in any organizational setting the individual must have opportunities to grow in order to feel satisfied. This is also true if an organization is to maintain and enhance its performance. Consequently, improving the individual's ability to respond creatively to problems or opportunities enhances organizational effectiveness. What is true of individuals seems to be true of organizations, they form and maintain.

We believe that there can be simultaneous and mutually reinforcing growth in both the individual and the organization. Everybody can "win" in building personal self-actualization and organizational effectiveness. In situations where mutual development is not the case—that is, when one or both parties lose—a high price is paid in human resources and dollars.

Many contemporary organizations exhibit structures and processes which would be characterized as immature and pathological in individuals. When individuals interact with parent-child mannerisms, neither individual nor organizational potential can be attained. This is exemplified when a superior requests compliance with a directive by hinting at the resulting application of rewards or sanctions, and the subordinate reacts in dependent or counter-dependent ways—unconditional submission or revolt. When conditions prevent individuals from trusting others enough to let their guard down or from feeling sufficiently secure in themselves to act autonomously, the capacity to learn from experience is diminished, and the individuals and the organizations stagnate instead of grow. When individuals accept the formal organizational structure as a reality, they are unable to perceive what is really happening. Consequently they are unable to see things objectively and cannot make creative contributions to the organization.

These conditions result in the dissipation of potentially useful energy as people "claw" their way to the top of the organization at the expense of others and the organization, or expend energy in other noncontributory ways, such as in worry and anxiety. These are not natural or healthy conditions. Fortunately, we have at least four ways in which to respond to these conditions or circumstances. We can decide to "cop-out" and passively accept the situation, perhaps "getting even" with the organization by covert actions. Or we can leave the organization to find a more compatible "fit" in another organization or in another department in the same organization. A third choice would be to remain in the organization and change our own perception of the situation or to modify our needs and values. The last option would be to stay in the organization and work actively to modify the organizational structure and climate to better "fit" our needs. Chapter 7 elaborates on these four choices and focuses on the skills involved in decision making.

OPPORTUNITIES FOR SELF-ACTUALIZATION WITHIN ORGANIZATIONS

If we feel a need to change and grow, it should be in directions of our choosing. Neither the type of change nor the actions required to bring it about will make sense until we get in touch with our private selves and become conscious of our values and needs. Many of us have only a vague sense of who we are and what we need and want from life. Intuitively or subconsciously we may have a fair idea of what our values are, but when it comes to understanding the values and structures of a particular organization we may be totally ignorant. Our feelings and bodily reactions tell us when there is a match or mismatch between our values and needs and the values and structure of our organization. We know this because of our feelings of satisfaction or dissatisfaction. Intelligent decision making requires a conscious awareness of not only our own values and needs, but also those of the organization. Chapters 2, 3, 5, and 6 focus on individual values and needs, organizational values and structures, and value-clarification and assessment skills.

In order to generate opportunities for self-development according to our internal priorities, we need a *Personal Development Strategy*—that is, a game plan which gives us direction and enough flexibility to achieve the kind of satisfaction we desire. This Strategy can help us to reevaluate and restructure our life so that we can take full advantage of our potential to achieve the self-actualization, satisfaction, and fulfillment we seek in our personal and organizational lives.

A *Personal Development Strategy* is a method for personalized, planned change, which consists of six steps:

1 Situational and organizational assessment
2 Personal assessment
3 Assessment of person-organization match-mismatch
4 Decision making
5 Commitment
6 Implementation and evaluation

Chapter 4 elaborates on these six steps and shows how to use this Strategy.

Given the perspective and strategy to analyze our circumstances and situations, we have the potential to turn crises and problems into growth opportunities. When we rechannel our negative reactions and feelings into positive directions, our psychic energy is not unnecessarily consumed in defensive behavior or psychosomatic symptoms and we begin to achieve and develop.

Unfortunately, we do not always take advantage of these opportunities to achieve and develop, even if we are aware of them and know how to influence them. There may be either external or internal barriers that prevent us from doing this.

BARRIERS TO SELF-ACTUALIZATION IN ORGANIZATIONS

The logic of organizational life has a conservative thrust. Often we would rather suffer the loss of opportunity for growth to maintain the security of an accustomed structure or process. It sometimes seems safer to accept a known condition with its imperfections than to gamble on possibly creating a worse situation.

It is also sometimes easier to "do nothing" than "do something," especially if doing something might create disorder. The need for stability and regularity is a commonly accepted condition of human life in organizations. In Joe Brennon's case, his "do-nothing" approach was not dealing effectively with the dissatisfaction he and the faculty were experiencing. In this case, other factors—either Joe's physical symptoms or the actions of the senior faculty—may force an unfavorable change unless a positive-change effort is somehow introduced.

An individual's change effort may encounter calculated opposition. Change is almost always perceived as affecting someone negatively. Those who feel threatened will resist, even if there is no certain negative result, because of the fear that the change might damage their interests. Even if this resistance could be overcome, the costs are often prohibitive.

Dick Larson was so fearful of what he perceived to be a negative change that he chose to withdraw from the situation completely rather than risk possible overpowering opposition. In this case, checking out the facts would have provided the data needed for a better, reality-based decision.

Psychic costs are also involved in change. It is hard to alter behavior. The initiator is anxious about the risks involved should the change fail. The initiator could suffer embarrassment, loss of status and influence, and maybe even position. The costs of behaving in old ways are at least known. The possible battles and resulting enemies, along with the necessary compromises that might be required, cause anxiety and detract from the estimated benefits of change efforts. Much stronger incentives exist which encourage one to act more "warily than daringly." Precedent serves as a valuable guide because it defines a safe path.

Through organization acculturation, individuals are socialized to "fit in." Values and perceptions are shaped with respect to desired behavior by means of the organization's support and maintenance systems. Well-known methods are utilized to weed out "misfits" and promotions indicate which of the attributes an individual possesses are most highly prized by superiors. Training programs teach individuals to do things the "right" way and organized activities solidify group norms. Hence, the conditions of the organization are accepted as a way of life and attempts to innovate are seen as disruptive and threatening. Unfortunately for people like Joe Brennon and for the university involved, the values attached to fitting social expectations often become more important than contributions to the organization's primary objectives.

These informal restraints are matters of accepted practice. They are just as binding but harder to detect and alter than official or external restraints. Resource limitations and formal rules are at least identifiable targets which can be attacked, and their progress can be measured. Informal restraints, group norms, and climate are often difficult to measure because they are less tangible. These dimensions of organizational structure and behavior are elaborated on in Chapters 3 and 6.

OVERCOMING BARRIERS TO SELF-ACTUALIZATION: BEING YOUR OWN CHANGE AGENT

We believe that most people can learn to assess (1) themselves (needs, aspirations, values, and level of development) and (2) their organization (its values and structures, as well as developmental level). Then, using models such as the Personal Development Strategy, they can make intelligent decisions about whether to "adjust" to work demands, to attempt to change the task environment, to leave the organization, or to change themselves.

You may ask, "How can you expect *me* to do anything? I'm not an organizational development specialist and, even if I were, I wouldn't be able to exercise any power or authority, especially in this kind of organization." It is true that most planned-change efforts in organizations are mediated by outside change agents, usually management consultants with doctorates in behavioral sciences. Occasionally, innovative organizations have a staff of internal change agents whose primary purpose is to plan, initiate, and evaluate planned-change programs. But it is also true that organizations are constantly changing, whether the change is planned or left to circumstance or chance. It is unrealistic to believe that all change—especially unplanned, unmeditated change—happens for the best, or that what is right for the organization is right for you, or conversely. Change needs direction!

Our point is simply this: You cannot wait for someone else, such as an outside consultant, to plan and execute change for you. It may be in your best interest to become *your own* change agent. This does not mean that you will necessarily have to take on the whole organization—although you might—but it does mean that you should examine that part of the organization in which you feel you can exert some degree of power or authority (even if it is only one or two functions in your department) and assess the feasibility of planned change.

It is becoming increasingly clear that we must take the responsibility for our working conditions in organizations. If we are dissatisfied with the conditions we find ourselves in, we can and should take a more active role in bringing about positive change, whether it be in ourselves or in the organization. Outside consultants may be experts in assessment and change techniques, but organizational members are more in touch with internal conditions. It is also true that the supply of qualified external change agents is disproportionately below the demand that organizations have for their services, even though they may not recognize their need. On the other hand, assessment and change skills are becoming increasingly available to the "lay" change agent through books, articles, seminars, and canned packages.

Today, nearly everyone with decision-making responsibility has the potential for being a change agent. What one needs is a realistic understanding of the development process as it relates to both the individual and the organization—a knowledge of the opportunities for self-actualization and organizational effectiveness, the skills for assessment and intervention, and a strategy (such as the Personal Development Strategy), which provides direction, encourages commitment, and provides constant feedback. The skills needed for changing self and organization are available to all, whether the organization concerns business, government, health, education, or family. Individuals equipped with the knowledge and skills presented in this book should be able to bring about a better integration of their own needs and the needs of the organization, thereby allowing for more satisfaction for the individual and more effective operation for the organization.

A WORD ABOUT SELF-ACTUALIZATION

In the past few years the term "self-actualization" has literally become a household word. It seems as though everyone uses the term self-actualization with a variety of meanings. These definitions range from "triumphing over a tough personal problem" to "doing your own thing" to "achieving nirvana." Unfortunately, these connotations of the term are very different from those proposed by psychologists and psychiatrists. Basically, these professionals do *not* view self-actualization as an attempt to achieve happiness or satisfaction. Rather, they view happiness and self-satisfaction as by-products of self-actualization.

Self-actualization is described as a process of realizing or actualizing values or, put another way, finding meaning in one's life. A person finds meaning in his or her life by being and becoming increasingly inner-directed and integrated with one's self and in relation to other people. Meaning in one's life can only be found by going beyond one's self and becoming a socially useful or self-transcendent person. It is only then that a person can experience feelings of happiness and self-satisfaction. This view of self-actualization is elaborated on in Chapter 4.

It should become clear to the reader throughout the next three chapters why we have focused on self-actualization in terms of values or meanings and why we have emphasized the interdependence between the person and his or her relationship with others, especially with the organization. In Chapters 2 and 3, you will learn about the process of growth and development for both individuals and organizations in terms of values, styles, and structures. In Chapter 4, we will discuss the meaning of self-actualization, the process of planned personal change, and the Personal Development Strategy.

Chapter 2

How Individuals Develop and Change

The organizational environment can either help or hinder an individual in achieving his or her immediate goals, as well as the long-range goals of finding fulfillment in life, or self-actualization. In this chapter we will see that an individual's progress toward short-term goals and life fulfillment can also be helped or hindered by personal characteristics. An individual's stage of development, value structure, and personality style combine to produce the capacity for obtaining job satisfaction, effective coping behavior, and openness to change. If these factors are out of balance, however, they can interact to produce a disgruntled, unhappy person who survives in the organization but contributes little to the organization's growth and productivity—in other words, the organization may not always be the culprit in cases of individual discontent.

The key to achieving a sense of self-satisfaction and control over our lives is understanding who we are—that is, "What are our needs, values, and goals?" Until we understand ourselves, we will not be able to establish a clear plan of action for solving our problems. Before we can establish our Personal Development Strategy, we need a firm understanding of how we develop and change. We can then better understand the part our stage of development plays in determining our current mix of values, goals, and satisfaction level.

Theories of human development and change have emphasized two primary methods of explaining human behavior: (1) comparing the behavior of a person to a standard of behavior held to be typical for others like him or her; and (2) attempting to understand the behavior of a person by gaining insight into how he or she perceives the experiences of life. The first method—*external* viewpoint or frame of reference—assesses what an observer sees in a person in comparison to others. The second method—*internal* viewpoint or frame of reference—assesses the individual's unique impression of self and environment as he or she perceives and interprets them.

Neither the external nor internal approach is right or wrong; they are merely different methods of generating information from two different sources. As we begin to understand ourselves, it becomes crucial that data from our environment be incorporated in the way we perceive our experiences. In studying how individuals develop and change, *both* viewpoints must be used. Figure 2.1 presents the three behavioral determinants we will describe in this chapter and the appropriate frame of reference for each.

Variables	Frame of reference	
	Internal	External
Stages of adult development		X
Values	X	
Personality style	X	X

Fig. 2.1. Frame of reference and behavior variables.

The three components—adult development, values, and personality style—incorporate both frames of reference and provide us with a comprehensive view of our behavior.

By comparing our behavior to that typical of other adults of a comparable age, we can determine whether our feelings of distress, tension, and satisfaction, for example, are common to feelings most adults experience at that stage in life. Recent research in *adult development* has suggested that there are certain events which usually are experienced by all of us at specific periods of time in our lives. Questioning of our basic life goals and beliefs begins anew whenever we start the transition from one stage of development to another. Each stage of adulthood has its own unique *values* or behavior patterns which we believe are desirable for ourselves and others. Our values are formed by our interaction with others and our environment, and they are defined by what we seek or achieve. Values influence our decisions and the way in which we lead our lives. They are unique to each individual and must be looked at from the individual's point of view.

In order to completely understand our behavior, a third component of our behavior determinants—*personality style*—must be considered. Our personality style is a reflection of our goals and the typical styles of behavior we use to achieve these goals. Our behavior forms a pattern with a central, unified theme which influences every aspect of our thoughts, feelings, and behavior. Insight into our personality style can help us understand why we act the way we do.

After we have looked at these three components in depth, we will apply the concepts to the four case studies referred to in Chapter 1 so that we can better understand the difficulties involved. We will then be in a better position to apply the concepts to our own lives and thus be better able to understand who we are, where we are going, and why.

STAGES OF ADULT DEVELOPMENT

A perusal of the traditional developmental psychology literature reveals that most psychologists conclude that personality growth and development seems to stop by the time we reach age 21. These theories emphasize the fact that most of our personality is formed by the time we reach 6 to 8 years of age; and the developmental process, though continuing through adolescence, is complete by the time we reach age 21. According to most of these psychologists, *adulthood is perceived as one vast area devoid of any significant development.*

Those of us who have passed our thirtieth birthday know that something significant has occurred in our lives. Achieving 40, 50, and 65 years of age carries with it a set of experiences and expectations which influence our families and job performance as well as our personal lives. Psychologists have only recently begun to scientifically investigate adulthood from a developmental viewpoint and to organize these experiences we have as maturing adults.

The usefulness of a developmental approach for understanding adult-life stages is based on two assumptions: First, one crucial dimension of individual difference is age. Different age groups have unique sets of behavioral configurations which differentiate them from each other. The emphasis is on the different kinds of behavior which seem necessary at different stages of our adult life. Second, each life stage involves characteristic developmental tasks which must be recognized, confronted, and mastered if future development is to proceed optimally.

Havighurst (1953), a developmental psychologist, has defined a developmental task as, "... a task which arises at or about a certain period in the life of the individual, successful achievement of which leads to happiness and to success with later tasks, while failure leads to unhappiness in the individual, disapproval by the society, and difficulty with later tasks."

Erik Erikson, the leading contemporary thinker in psychoanalytic theory and human development, was the first professional to look at human development as a process which continues throughout life. He states that because there is a total interaction between a person and his or her environment throughout life, personality growth and change cannot be restricted to the first 20 years. He divided the life cycle into eight stages—four to cover the first 20 years of life and four to include the rest of life. Each stage is distinct and unique with its own particular problems and needs. Each stage presents the individual with a major task to be achieved if a healthy personality is to proceed.

Erikson's work has provided a theoretical basis for research into the stages of adult development. Two researchers who have provided empirical evidence to support the contention that adult life is a series of stages which can be delineated and described are Daniel Levinson at Yale University and Roger Gould at the University of California at Los Angeles. Their research presents solid evidence that adulthood is a time of continuing psychological development which can be divided into some fairly identifiable stages.

At a symposium at Hunter College in March, 1973, Daniel Levinson presented a paper entitled, "Normal Crises of the Middle Years," in which he states that there is an order to the developmental course of life with specific age spans for each period, and he prescribes developmental tasks which must be successfully mastered. A person can expect periods when his or her particular life structure is forming, periods when it is breaking up and changing, and periods when it is stable. Many obstacles occur and many changes take place within each period, but an individual can move on to the next stage only after he or she starts working on new developmental tasks and building a new structure for his or her life. According to Levinson, no structure lasts longer than 7 to 10 years.

Roger Gould, writing in *Psychology Today* (February, 1975), reported that the evolution of a personality continues through the fifth decade of life. His research touches on the process of formation which continues through our adult life. He states that during the years of adulthood, there is an increasing need to win permission from oneself to continue developing, through a process which he calls "thoughtful confrontation." Most of us become adults with images of what we *should* be like, how successful we *should* be, and how we *should* be able to do the impossible. An adult who does not confront these "shoulds" lives a life controlled by impossible attempts to satisfy expectations based upon a child's point of view. Consequently, it is necessary to confront and dispense with these "shoulds" before we can be free to develop our unique selves.

Gail Sheehy (1976) has combined Gould's and Levinson's work with her own research and has established a scheme for describing the ages and stages of adult development. The stages and tasks are summarized below.

Pulling Up Roots (Ages 16 to 22)

Until reaching age 18 the major theme is, "I have to get away from my parents." However, very seldom does the "getting away" occur. At this age a person is more a family member than an individual. The future seems vague and family security is subject to change.

The new reality which must be confronted is that it is time to become more than a member of the family. It becomes crucial for the person to sort out his or her attitudes and opinions and to be distinguished from the parents. After age 18 the cleavage line between the family and person widens. The individual is on the borderline between a family and a personal base. There is a push-pull tendency and a fear of not being able to completely make it. Despite protests to the contrary, the individual's belief system is nearly indistinguishable from his or her family's because of the lack of experience in living outside the family.

The peer group takes on a supporting role, yet is also regarded as a threat. If the peer group cannot soothe or support the individual as the family has done or if the group's thinking is not identical to the individual's, it is seen as a betrayer. Autonomy is desired but is jeopardized by both peers and parents.

People who marry during this period are often seeking a partner to replace the family's supportive role, while those who must start earning a living to support themselves often prolong ties to the family and relatives. Not achieving autonomy during this stage prevents a person from becoming self-sufficient. Those who do not achieve self-sufficiency during this period run the risk of underperforming in careers or being bound to their families.

Provisional Adulthood (Ages 22 to 29)

The first attempts at becoming an adult begin during Provisional Adulthood. It is a time to build a life system of one's own and move beyond family, school, service, or travel. Early in this period, individuals insist that what they are doing is their true course in life and they waste little time evaluating commitments. The fears of still being children and being unable to fend for themselves persist; these fears may continue into the 40's, presenting additional evidence that development continues beyond age 21.

The tasks of this period are to explore the possibilities for work, personal relationships, and memberships in society. Visions of oneself, which can later be converted into goals, are formed. Doing what one "should" becomes the strongest theme of this period. If the prevailing culture says "get married," you get married! If it says "do your own thing," you do it!

One of the major fears experienced during the 20's is a sense of our decisions being irrevocable. Whether we choose to go to graduate school, get a job, move, travel, or explore, we will be locked in. Two impulses are at work—one is to build a safe future by making firm commitments and the other is to explore and experiment and remain tentative. How these impulses are integrated and balanced define how a person passes through Provisional Adulthood.

Provisional Adults who chose stability will make strong commitments and will defend what they have chosen as the true course. By choosing with intensity, they move toward self-authority faster. If they feel "locked in" at age 30, some will use this transition period to "break out." Those who do not break out will have the hardest time in their 40's.

Age-30 Transition (Ages 29 to 32)

The bubble of optimism characteristic of Provisional Adults bursts during the Age-30 Transition. At the end of the 20's, there is a definite new sense of time. Questions arise concerning one's commitment to the choices made during the previous stage. "Now that I am doing what I am supposed to do, what is this life all about?" Impatient with what we "should" be doing, we begin to ask, "What do I want out of life?" Being selfish becomes a right and a need during the early 30's. To some, this is just a vague feeling of restlessness. For others it means, "I've worked hard and I deserve more; something has been missing."

The Provisional Adult now enters into a transitional stage which will prepare the foundation for the next stage, Rooting. Choices and commitments must be made and making choices involves great change, unrest, and crises. A common occurrence during the Age-30 Transition is the destruction of a life one has spent most of his or her 20's putting together. Often divorce occurs or at least a serious questioning of marriage. The spouse is often regarded as preventing or failing to recognize the emergence of our new self and a desire to be accepted for "what we are!"

Rooting (Ages 32 to 39)

A settling-down process occurs for the first time during the early 30's. Self-questioning changes its tone. There is an increasing awareness of a "time-squeeze" with an eye cast equally to the past, present, and future. There are two early tasks recognized during this period: (1) to become acknowledged as a junior member of one's occupation, and (2) to set a timetable that will assist in shaping the individual's wishes into concrete, long-term goals. However, with the focus almost entirely on external goals, life during this stage can be boring; more so than during any other stage.

The "time-squeeze" hits at age 35. It is no longer enough to be the promising young professor or the junior executive with potential—like the promising athlete whose potential is always a year away, we suddenly realize there are not many years left. Recognition for what one *is* becomes a primary concern—a professor with talent and skill in his or her own right; a junior executive who becomes a part of management. With some anger, the individual discovers that he or she has been too anxious to please *others* during this time frame because of a need for recognition.

From 35 to 39, the desire to put our ship in order becomes a primary concern. Movement towards becoming our own person, less dependent on external praise and less vulnerable to criticism, characterizes our behavior.

By the time we reach age 40, we are struck by a simple, shattering fact: "My life is half over." The process of "growing up" has ended and has been replaced by the process of "growing old." A paradox confronts us at this point in life. At the time when we should be experiencing feelings of great enjoyment and fulfillment, we become aware that death is inevitable. This paradox may send us in search of "one last chance to make it big."

While it is impossible to predict what career a person will be in or how successful he or she will be at age 30, by the time age 40 arrives, a clear picture of what has been achieved will emerge. If a person has been successful, he or she must find a way not to stagnate within this success. If a person has fallen short, he or she must lower these goals and find an alternative for maintaining a feeling of worth.

Mid-life Transition (Ages 39 to 43)

The 40's actually seem to begin in the late 30's, and the transitional period is a time of intense discomfort. The gap between childhood's dreams and adult achievement must be confronted. The task during this period is to find ways of connecting the parts of self not provided for in the old life system. The fantasy of "what I would like to be" needs to be integrated into "what I am."

With an awareness of the "time-squeeze," the question becomes, "Is there time to change?" This question applies to the individual as well as to his or her family. An awareness that the children are quickly developing autonomy; that one's parents are again turning toward him or her and provoking old feelings of dependency versus independency; and that one's spouse is looking for support all create a sense of quiet desperation. Work is often looked on as the hoped for compensation for all of this and, in an illusory way, of offering "one last chance to make it big."

Again, as with the Age-30 Transition, an individual may make decisions which break the well-established base lines created during his or her lifetime. Marriage may be terminated; career aspirations may change. The Mid-life Transition marks the last point at which *dramatic* life changes tend to occur.

Restabilization and Flowering (Ages 43 to 50)

The early 40's are an unstable and uncomfortable time because of a desperate feeling of having to make an impact on the world, while in the late 40's a marked stabilization process takes place. As Erikson pointed out, this period is the one most elderly people remember with fondness. The person who has successfully created a life system out of the experiences of earlier years feels that this is the best time of his or her life.

Finite time is accepted as a reality which cannot be changed or modified by self-illusion. Relief from the turmoil of earlier years is experienced in a "die-is-cast" feeling. The stabilization process is accompanied by a closing-off process. The task during this period is to contain the anger and bitterness that comes with the acceptance of being a separate person and mortal.

A new stability is achieved with the acceptance of the new

order of things. Life is even! It may be more or less satisfying than before but it is stable. There is a possibility of achieving true autonomy from the external world by deciding to listen to the "delicate striving" of the self, as contained in one's own unique life, which can only be lived in one's own unique way.

Mellowing (Ages 50 to 60+)

During this stage a mellowing accompanies the feeling that, "I will try to be satisfied with what I have and not to think so much about the things I probably won't be able to do." There is increasing concern about health and an increasing agreement that, "I can't do things as well as I used to."

As the life span shortens, little concern is given for the future. Accompanying this attitude is a renewed questioning of the meaningfulness of life as well as a review of one's contributions to this world. Relationships are less substantive and discussions lead away from emotional-laden topics. Petty annoyances begin to dominate conversations, along with health-related topics.

A summary of the stages and tasks of adult development is presented in Fig. 2.2. It is important to remember that these descriptions of adult development are general and reflect averages. Differences are dependent upon individual life style, personality structure, and subculture. The common denominator of the changes which we as adults experience is what we face *not* how we face it.

Times of crisis, depression, and stress are usually attributed to external events, such as divorce, job loss, tedious work, or bad working conditions. A small percentage of the population attribute the causes of their pain to something inside themselves which they simply have to ride out. Fewer still will be able to understand that there may be no external causes and yet their difficulties may take several years to resolve. In situations like these, knowledge of the tasks of adulthood would be helpful in dealing with the stresses and crises of a particular age span. Indeed, much of the discomfort caused by these crises is the normal "stuff of development" and is not unique to any individual.

In summary, as Roger Gould (1972) has stated, children mark the passing years by observing their changing bodies, while adults

Stages	Task
1. Pulling-up roots (ages 16–22)	Autonomy Self-sufficiency
2. Provisional adulthood (ages 22–29)	Select a career Establish personal relationships Achieve a place in society
3. Age-30 transition (ages 29–32)	Search for personal identity Reassess future objectives Search for meaning in life
4. Rooting (ages 32–39)	Establish long-term goals Receive recognition in career/career success
5. Mid-life transition (ages 39–43)	Confrontation of gap between aspirations and achievement Reexamination of career Reexamination of personal relationships
6. Restabilization and flowering (ages 43–50)	Acceptance of time as finite Confrontation of mortality Autonomy
7. Mellowing (ages 50–60+)	Acceptance of what I have Fewer personal relationships Examination of present and what it means

Fig. 2.2. Stages and tasks of adult development.

change their minds. Experiences and events build up pressure during our lives until energy is somehow released, thereby altering relationships with both time and people. By recognizing these patterns in our lives, we may be able to gain some control over these forces and smooth out the transitional process.

VALUES AND BEHAVIOR

Every day we face situations which demand an opinion, a decision, or some type of action. Everything we do is a reflection of our attitudes, beliefs, and values. The ways in which we demonstrate our values may be unique and a reflection of our individual creativity, but there is no doubt that our behavior is a reflection of what we value.

Values are beliefs and attitudes that we feel are desirable for ourselves and others and are reflected in our behavior. The family life, peer groups, cultural influences, and crises of life we experience influence our value structure. Values account for the *satisfaction* we feel as a result of *how* we satisfy our needs. Values also refer to the worth and the results of an activity rather than to any functional pleasure gained from engaging in that activity.

Given the multitude of potential values in our culture, it is understandable that we experience value conflicts. Our values are largely shaped and formed in the context of societal norms; but given the rapidity at which change occurs and the variety of inputs we receive, there is little wonder that we are not sure of what we "think" we should value and what we "should" value.

If we try to model ourselves after the values of the media, we may find that we are caught in a state of perpetual motion. Likewise, if we try to emulate current trends, we are left dizzy by their constant change. While looking for clues as to what we should value, we are in danger of becoming "searchers" or those who look outside of self for answers. Our behavior would then be in response to external standards and expectations rather than in response to our internal needs.

According to Robert Havighurst (1953), values can be classified in two categories—instrumental activities and expressive activities—which are distinguishable by the kind of activity they lead people to favor. Havighurst's classification scheme is helpful in understanding the nature of the changes in our society which can produce value conflicts. *Instrumental activity* is a means to an end outside of the activity, while *expressive activity* has engaging in the activity itself as the goal. For example, if we decide to enroll in a course in order to qualify for a salary increase or a promotion, we are engaging in an instrumental activity. If we decide to enroll in a course at the local university for the "fun of it," we are engaging in an expressive activity.

Expressive values seem to be emerging in our society, while

instrumental values are receding. This transition has influenced our behavior, our beliefs, and our attitudes. William Glasser, writing in *The Identity Society* (1972), describes the change as moving from goals to roles. Goals are future-oriented and are payoffs for successfully completing prescribed activities. The task takes precedence over our needs and feelings. Goals and instrumental activities can be equated. Roles are those behaviors which provide an identity for us. Our identity is a function of the activities we are engaged in. Roles are processes—i.e., doing-oriented—while goals are outcomes and are what we work toward. Roles can be equated with expressive activities.

The television industry has been aware of the changing focus from goals (instrumental activities) to roles or identity (expressive activities) for over 25 years. Their awareness of roles and identity has enabled them to sell items of no utility, as well as items of negative value, such as cigarettes. To be a hit with the opposite sex all we need to do is use the right toothpaste and effective deodorant and drink the proper beer. Slogans identifying us with particular products are aimed at helping us to achieve the "right" identity.

The following chart presents some of the instrumental values that are receding and expressive values which are emerging:

EXAMPLES OF RECEDING AND EMERGING VALUES

Instrumental	Expressive
(Receding)	(Emerging)
Work as the principal basis of self-worth	Individual activities (doing your own thing) as source of identity
Acceptance of authority	Respond to actions not symbols
Future-oriented—tolerate prolonged hardships	Here-and-now oriented—demand immediate satisfaction
Compromise values for success	Honesty in behavior and relationships
Competition and conflict	Cooperation and collaboration

The rapidity with which change occurs in our society, the variety of external demands, and the tasks that confront developing adults contain the necessary ingredients for producing stress and tension in our lives. Within each stage of our development, normative behaviors occur. Entry into each stage is characterized by our present value system being challenged by the tasks of the new stage. Selecting and choosing a behavior to cope with the life task is a function of our own unique value structure. Our coping behavior interacts with the life task to bring about a change in our values. To help us through the turmoil of change, a knowledge of what each stage demands from us and a knowledge of our individual value systems can assist us in facilitating a successful resolution of the life task.

In dealing with our life tasks, many potential alternatives are available to us. Knowing what we want and need to do is not quite the same as deciding which option is best. Often, we need to make compromises based upon our value judgments. These value judgments determine how we mobilize our resources to master our environment and become creative, need-fulfilled individuals.

Robert Carkhuff and Ted Friel (1974) offer a scheme for helping us to organize our values, thus making them clear to us. They divide values into three types: physical, emotional, and intellectual.

Physical values involve activities which we physically perform or those which have a physical effect on us. For example, travel, body use, and body conditioning require physical activity. Working and living conditions have a physical effect on us.

Emotional values involve our ideas and the attitudes we have concerning ourselves and other people. Intimacy, love, compassion, openness, and commitment are examples of emotional values.

Intellectual values relate to our cognitive processes. Creativity, wisdom, perfection, competition, and independence are examples of intellectual values.

Figure 2.3 presents a representative list of values, common to the physical, emotional, and intellectual domains, which is intended to start you thinking about what values are important to you and to prepare you for the value identification process in Chapter 5.

Values have an impact on our job satisfaction. Values influence how involved in or committed to our jobs we are. Research has

Physical	Emotional	Intellectual
activity	responsibility	learning
body use	stability	creativity
comfort	prestige	complexity
travel	competition	decision making
appearance	commitment	computation
money/reward	equality	abstraction
vacation	security	accomplishment
prosperity	trust	wisdom
strength	intimacy	independence
health	caring	rational
attractiveness	love	perfection
privacy	friendliness	planning
living conditions	compassion	reading
working conditions	openness	communication
body conditioning	involvement	completion

Fig. 2.3. Physical, emotional, and intellectual values.

found that job satisfaction is positively related to the degree of agreement between job conditions and personal values. Also, the more important the values involved, the greater their impact on job satisfaction, either positively or negatively. (And job satisfaction varies according to the values of the workers.) Finally, different levels of job satisfaction among people having similar values are associated with differences in their occupations. It seems clear that when there is a match between a worker's values and the work he or she is required to perform, the worker is happier and is able to contribute to the success of the organization. Conversely, a mismatch between a person's values and the organization's values contributes to dissatisfaction and low productivity.

Thus far we have seen how developmental tasks help us to understand our behavior with respect to what we have in common with other people at similar stages in their lives. Values help us identify what is uniquely important to us and what contributes to our specific happiness. The concept of personality style provides us with an understanding of why we act the way we do to achieve those tasks according to our values.

DEVELOPMENT OF A PERSONALITY STYLE

The concept of using a personality style to describe the behaviors we utilize to achieve our life's goals is based on the work of Alfred Adler, a Viennese psychiatrist. While Adler used the term "style of life," we have borrowed the term "personality style" from the writings of Len Sperry and Lee Hess (1974) in their book, *Contact Counseling*.

Our personality styles are unique. They develop to help us achieve our life's goals. Our basic goals are to belong, to be accepted, and to actualize our potential. How we set about to achieve our goals contributes to our personality style. Knowing what our goals are helps us to understand why we act the way we do.

The behaviors we engage in to achieve our goals develop early in life—in fact, our early experiences as infants have a profound impact on behavior. Each stimulus is new and significant to infants. How our parents and significant others attended to us, phychologically and physically, and the emotional climate of our home environment influenced how we grew and developed. Other variables which influence our development are birth order, family size, and sex. The myriad experiences we have as we develop combine to form our self-concept, how we perceive others around us, and how we perceive life.

Most of the impressions, thoughts, and feelings we have about ourselves, others, and our environment are developed by the time we reach age five or six. By that age, we have made decisions about ourselves—how we feel about being "me," and how we feel about life. From these decisions our dominate goal or what we need to achieve to be satisfied is formed, and the kinds of behavior we will use to achieve that goal are selected.

Based on the writings of humanistic psychologists and our experiences, we have identified six basic personality styles which tend to characterize and describe behavior. In Fig. 2.4 we have displayed the six styles in the form of a personality-style continuum. Each personality style contains an unhealthy as well as a healthy dimension. Most of us exhibit different combinations of the basic personality styles.

As well as containing an unhealthy/healthy dimension, each per-

Psychologically unhealthy (Lo synergy)	Psychologically healthy (Hi synergy)
Driver	Achiever
Inadequate One	Adequate One
Martyr	Courageous One
Right One	Fair One
Getter	Helper
Controller	Leader

Fig. 2.4. Personality-style continuum.

sonality style contains a lo-synergy/hi-synergy dimension. Synergy stresses a process whereby we are able to release the creative process we possess. Synergy focuses on the positive attributes each of us has developed and stresses that growth is possible when all the components of our behavior configuration are harmoniously developed. Each behavior pattern is blended and integrated without any particular characteristic dominating the scene and preventing the integration from occurring. *Synergy* literally means an integrated whole which is larger than the sum of its parts. When the integration occurs, a healthy personality style with a hi-synergy level is developed.

Unhealthy personality styles contain lo-synergy levels. The integration of individuals' growth potential is blocked when "they lose the courage to be." Their being is threatened wherever they turn and their behavior thus develops a reactive, defensive position to its environment. In Chapter 8 we will talk more about our growth potential and our striving for self-actualization.

Now let us look at the six personality styles and we will briefly describe the healthy and unhealthy dimensions. In Chapter 5, you will have an opportunity to develop your own unique *Personality-style Profile*.

The Driver

The *Driver* is a "workaholic," an overachiever, a person who puts in an eight day work week! This type of person has an uncontrollable need to work and perform constantly. Drivers are never satisfied with their accomplishments and are rarely able to enjoy the numerous experiences of success they have. The goal of a Driver is to prove self-worth by successfully completing each task with which he or she is presented. By being successful, the Driver will become a worthy person. However, the big problem is that for the Driver the tasks are endless; there are always five more to replace the one just completed. Generally, Drivers experience feelings of emptiness. Something is missing! So they work harder. Drivers are thus caught in a vicious circle which soon becomes apparent to everyone.

The Achiever

The *Achiever* works just as hard as the driver but this individual is different. When the Achiever has successfully completed a task, he or she can relax and enjoy what was accomplished. Achievers take pride in their work and yet can relax and enjoy doing nothing. Generally, Achievers feel good about themselves and others and believe in what they are doing. Achievers work well with others and are able to maximize their talents.

The Inadequate One

The *Inadequate One* is convinced that he or she is helpless. Everything Inadequate Ones touch will self-destruct. These individuals are underachievers, who are sure to fail when given any responsibility. Inadequate Ones constantly need supervision and do not believe in their abilities. The need to depend on others is so great that Inadequate Ones cannot allow themselves to succeed in any task and become masters at getting other people to do their work for them.

The Adequate One

The *Adequate One* acknowledges the strengths that he or she possesses and is also able to recognize his or her limitations. Adequate Ones do not feel threatened when they have to refuse tasks which they know they cannot perform adequately. When tasks match the strength of Adequate Ones, they are able to work alone and follow through on their assignments. Only minimal supervision is needed, as Adequate Ones work well with other people and pull their own weight.

The Martyr

The *Martyr* is ready to "die for a cause." Martyrs spend a great deal of time searching for injustices which they can claim for themselves. Their "poor-me" attitude and behavior is intended to attract sympathy from others and to increase their feelings of being victims. Ready to abdicate their position at the slightest challenge, Martyrs then "die for a cause."

The Courageous One

The *Courageous One* accepts people as they are and is able to risk presenting new ideas and innovative suggestions. While some of these ideas may not be accepted, Courageous Ones respect the opinions of others and do not feel "put down" by them. Able to challenge ideas, Courageous Ones do not engage in any destructive behavior designed to psychologically harm an opponent.

The Right One

The *Right One* can be best described as the "Monday-morning quarterback." This individual thrives on second-guessing and judges other peoples' decisions as being uninformed and wrong. Judgmental behavior serves to place the Right One in a position of superiority. He or she avoids making mistakes and will rationalize a "way out" when one does occur. The Right One goes to great lengths to persuade other people they were wrong.

The Fair One

The *Fair One* does not spend time blaming people or telling them "I knew you were going to fail!" Rather than judging others, the Fair One spends his or her time trying to figure out what went wrong and what can be done about it.

The Getter

The *Getter* believes that the world revolves around him or her. Getters feel that they are "entitled" to whatever they need or want, and Getters will actively or passively put others in their service to help them get what they are "entitled" to. They may use charm, flattery, subtle or direct manipulation, or slighted feelings to get what they want. Getters need the help of others because their "getting" is insatiable and they cannot "get" all they want by themselves. The Getter's need to "get" can never be satisfied.

The Helper

The *Helper* cares for others as well as self. Helpers are able to be supportive when necessary and are able to receive support with a sense of self-satisfaction. They believe that life is to be shared and are generally sought out as a friend by their colleagues. This behavior serves to enhance the emotional unity of those around the Helper.

The Controller

The *Controller* dislikes surprises, spontaneity, and/or the display of feelings as these qualities are not godlike. The Controller needs to control everything and everyone around him or her. There is a rule and procedure to govern everything. Things are to be done this way. If something does not go the Controller's way or as planned, he or she will jump in and come to the rescue. Adept at keeping subordinates in an inferior position, the Controller is not willing to recognize individual strengths or to share authority. The Controller will often engineer crises so he can play "hero," and show others his godlikeness.

The Leader

The *Leader* is a developer of people. This individual believes that people should participate in decisions and share in the responsibility of what happens. The Leader is spontaneous, creative, and likes to try new ways of doing things. Leaders believe everyone should learn from their experiences whether they are successful or not.

An individual's personality style becomes evident in behavior as it guides his or her actions. A person will act in a repetitive manner which confirms personality style. A circular pattern occurs giving rise to a self-fulfilling prophecy. Thus the apparent self-destructive behavior of an individual can be explained by the unifying factor of his or her life, dominant goal, or what is needed to survive and be satisfied.

The six personality styles and their opposites are descriptions of *pure extremes*. Most of us are not at one end of the continuum or the other, but somewhere in-between. You should also remember that our behavior may reflect a combination of two or more personality styles.

PUTTING IT ALL TOGETHER

Dick Larson, age 39, inventor of the electron pacifier, resigned in a state of confusion because he did not know how to deal with Fred Steggart or what to say to his supervisor. Joe Brennon, age 32, was distressed because he did not fit in the university structure. Ron Samuels, age 30, was having marital problems. Jean Lawrence, age 28, was unhappy in her position as a market research manager. Each of these cases will be elaborated on below to show how developmental stages, values, and personality styles interact.

Dick Larson's developmental tasks bordered on two stages—Rooting and Mid-life Transition. He had spent several years developing the electron pacifier, making a spot for himself as a member of the research team, becoming a project manager, and holding a position of influence at Lakeside Laboratories. However, his achievements in the intellectual domain did not eliminate his emotional need for respect and consideration, as he saw it. Combining his need for respect and consideration with the Inadequate-One side of his personality style, it is easy to see why Dick did not stand up for himself, but instead chose to quietly resign.

Joe's tasks of questioning his career and his current position and wondering whether or not he should change placed him in the Age-30 Transition stage, which is characterized by turmoil and change. Joe's values—being recognized, respected, and cared for by his colleagues—were not being met. His values concerning his family and the community provide him with emotional support, but without a job, he could lose it all. Joe's feelings of helplessness stemmed from the Inadequate-One portion of his personality style. However, Joe's Achiever and Courageous One may work to his advantage and overcome his inertia. It is unclear what Joe will do but it is apparent he will have to decide soon because of the effect indecision is having on his physical condition.

Ron is experiencing a reassessment of his marital situation—a common task for persons in the Age-30 Transition stage of development. His values of intellectual achievement and career success placed him in conflict with his wife. Ron's personality style of the Right One/Achiever became evident when he attempted to change his wife to the way he wanted her and did not attempt to see her from her perspective. He knows what is needed to make the marriage better, but has not taken Janet's views into consideration in his attempts to "save" the marriage. If he continues in the same direction, Ron is bound to fail.

Jean took her position at SOK soon after graduation from college. Her skills and talents enabled her to be promoted to Market Research Manager. However, she valued being independent, creative, and responsible to herself. Jean's development placed her in the Age-30 Transition stage, where she was reassessing her future objectives and searching for an identity to fit the type of career she wanted. Her personality-style profile reflected an Achiever, an Adequate One, and a Courageous One. Based on this information, it is understandable that Jean wanted to talk with her supervisor, assert her needs and wants, determine what was available in the interior design field, and then resign her position at SOK.

All four of these cases are characterized by a disparity between individual and organizational needs. Where there is a mismatch, there is dissatisfaction. We discussed in this chapter three components which influence our behavior. Our behaviors are partially determined by the tasks we need to achieve at particular stages of our development as adults. These tasks appear regardless of organizational setting or personal responsibilities. Satisfying the task may help solve the mismatch. Our behaviors are also reflected by our values. Our values show us what is important and contribute to how we decide to achieve it. Our personality style reflects what

predominant behavior patterns we utilize to achieve our goals. On an individual basis, these three areas help us to identify what we must do to develop our potential, what we need to be satisfied, and how we behave to achieve it.

In Chapter 5 we will offer you a diagnostic scheme for assisting you in identifying "where you are at." But first we need to step back and take a look at your organizational setting. Organizations, like individuals, develop and change. And that is what Chapter 3 is all about.

Chapter 3

How Organizations Grow and Develop

Organizational development, like individual development, can best be conceptualized as a continuous process with fairly identifiable stages. An organization experiences periods of change and stability with corresponding alterations in structure, resources, and opportunities—so does the individual. As soon as an organization solves the crises of its current structure, it moves on to its next developmental stage—so does the individual. Changes can result from forces in the environment or outside the boundaries of the organization, or from pressures developed within it. Consequently, we must continuously be aware of the interdependence of changes in the organization's external environment, internal structure, climate, and behavioral reactions.

It is important to understand the characteristics of organizational development so that we can assess the values and payoffs in our work situation. Such an assessment can increase our awareness and understanding of conditions such as what the organization expects and demands from us, what it enforces or lets go by, what it can truly provide in terms of rewards, punishments, and opportunities, and what personal-need satisfactions it promotes or hinders. These and other important organizational characteristics will be discussed in this chapter to provide you with a conceptual framework for assessing and evaluating your organization.

Since we are primarily concerned with organizational growth and development as it affects individual growth and development, it seems most appropriate to think of growth as increases in assets and employment levels, and development as changes in organization structure, climate, and behavioral patterns. Although age is usually correlated with development, some organizations, like some individuals, develop earlier than others. Our main concern is for the opportunities for individual growth and development provided by the organization through increases in size (growth) and corresponding changes in structure, climate, and expected behavior patterns.

FORCES ON THE ORGANIZATION TO GROW AND DEVELOP

Even though an organization uses methods such as training, rewards, rule enforcement, morale building, and other methods to preserve stable organizational patterns, it still cannot give everyone what they want. Consequently, social scientists have determined that it is a basic property of organizations to move toward those methods which offer maximum growth and development. In fact, Northcote Parkinson (1957) has noted that this tendency increases positions and personnel even when there is no accompanying increase in productivity. Why does this *maximization principle* seem so prevalent? Why do organizations continually strive to grow rather than secure and enjoy the stability they have accomplished? Some of the forces sustaining this growth-maximizing tendency are elaborated below.

Profit Profit can be broadly defined as "the difference between the value of services performed and the costs of these services." This concept is applicable to more than just business organizations. The "profit" from governmental agencies, hospitals, unions, and so forth, is measured by society because, if there is "no profit" from such organizations and if they cost more than they are worth, they disappear. Churches, for example, depend on voluntary contributions and, if the "take" is not sufficient, they "fail." Cost per unit decreases as the size of the organization increases due to the full utilization of specialists, lower costs of dealing with larger quantities, and increased efficiency of associated production technologies. Consequently, increasing size is a strategy often used to maximize profits.

Conflict resolution Internal strain inevitably occurs because of the inability of any organizational design to meet all the demands placed upon it. According to organizational psychologists, a typical way of dealing with internal conflict is compromise. Compromise tends to make concessions to subgroups rather than give up essential resources. The tendency is not to cut back on one subgroup but to upgrade the other. Consequently, because of the forces existing for self-preservation, it is an easy method for management to meet internal problems by expanding. The more patching up the organization does to keep going, the larger it becomes. In universities, for example, academic departments often ask for new courses or programs, stating that the existing personnel can handle them. After the new programs are started, however, the common "discovery" is that new budgets and personnel are required.

Another familiar political maneuver is to create a new committee rather than abolish an old one, or to increase the size of a committee to immobilize powerful members. This is an effective covert method of absorbing stress-producing members or subgroups in order to reduce their power by creating a larger structure. Since creating a larger structure is easier than eliminating members or subgroups, this method is also a growth-producing force.

Expansion is also a direct method of coping with the conflicts generated by a changing external environment. Cyert and March (1963), in *A Behavioral Theory of the Firm*, suggest that "co-opting" external sources of strain into the organization is an effective way of gaining control over them. Since organizations are not self-contained, they attempt to gain control over vital input and output markets, thus co-opting threatening organizations and creating resource-procuring structures.

Organizations may also take on new objectives, thereby causing the creation of new functions and structures to meet new demands. The United States government's policy of creating new agencies rather than eliminating old ones illustrates how organizations do survive and grow by acquiring new activities, structures, and personnel without letting old ones go.

Personal prestige, power, and job security Personal prestige, power, and job security are objectives that can be obtained through expansion. There is a certain amount of prestige attached to supervising large numbers of people, and it is accompanied by increased power, job security, and increased salary, because of the greater responsibility this position entails. Consequently, the tendency to increase personnel is not based on organizational needs, but rather on satisfying personal motives for security, prestige, achievement, power, and the like. The more the organization grows, the more resources and opportunities there are available for meeting personal needs.

A related motive that is perhaps more applicable to top executives than to the entire organization is the desire for adventure or risk taking, and "playing the game" for its own sake. This motive may permeate the organization by way of personnel who have mastered their tasks and seek change in an effort to avoid boredom. However, the main impetus for organizational growth inherent in this ideology is probably the top executives who feel compulsions to gamble on new activities in order to create adventure and risk.

Organizational ideologies In the American culture there is a positive value attached to bigness and growth. Consequently, an organizational ideology is that organizations should grow and expand in order to "justify their existence." In a competitive environment, organizational members may feel that their organization must grow faster and bigger than other organizations. This is a motive similar to those held by members of "true" religious faiths or "correct" political doctrines.

According to Bob Dylan, "He who is not busy being born is busy dying." A similar belief is that if organizations do not expand they contract. In other words, organizations cannot stand still—they must grow or die. As opposed to this defensive analogy, another more humanistic ideology is that organizations, like individuals, should continually strive to utilize their fullest potentials, which most often means expanding. This ideology can be thought of as "organizational self-realization."

FORCES ON THE ORGANIZATION TO RESIST GROWTH AND DEVELOPMENT

Because organizational change represents growth and because growth brings with it a host of associated changes, it is important to understand the reasons and forms of resistance to change. This, of course, assumes that pressures for growth and change are activated. One overriding reason for a lack of interest in growth and development would be the absence of pressures for these changes. Situations in which the previously mentioned forces toward growth do not exist would be those where there is no competition with similar organizations and where restricting the number of members increases the privileges and powers enjoyed. Under these conditions, there will be resistance to growth. Examples of such situations are skilled trade unions and the medical profession, both act to restrict the number of new members allowed to enter the organizations.

If the organization operates in an environment which harbors the pressures to grow, there still exist several barriers to change which function to block expansion. These barriers often operate even when the changes would be in the best interests of the organization and its members. These barriers can be grouped in three broad categories: (1) benefits of stability, (2) calculated opposition to change, and (3) inability to change.

Benefits of Stability

Organizational changes imply a modification of salaries, status, procedures, and behaviors. Consequently, even changes that might have significant long-term benefits incur the opposition of groups and individuals who feel that they may lose something. The logic of collective life has a conservative thrust. Why gamble on established, although imperfect, order for possible disorder? What exists may have its defects, but disruption of ongoing regularities could be even worse. The Declaration of Independence states that, "mankind are more disposed to suffer, while evils are sufferable, than to right themselves by abolishing the forms to which they are accustomed." Also it is easier to do nothing than to do something.

Calculated Opposition to Change

Attempts to change are almost always certain to encounter obstacles from the organized resistance of individuals and groups inside and/or outside the organization. When the intangible benefits of the prevailing system are considered (e.g., status, influence, security, sentiments, etc.), it is rare that any change can avoid being perceived by some as threatening their interests. Even if the harmful results cannot be specifically identified, anxiety often develops concerning the possible negative consequences which cannot be foreseen. People sometimes resist when they know the change will not harm them, in order to demand concessions for their acquiescence. Consequently, any change will almost always provoke organized resistance by those who deem themselves to be disadvantaged by it, even if the impact is not immediate or concrete.

Protecting quality is another common basis for resistance, be it in either the public interest or self-interest; and it is loudly vocalized in educational institutions (e.g., open enrollment or elimination of grading) and medical organizations (e.g., opposition to accepting practitioners of naturopathic disciplines), as well as in legal, religious, and business organizations.

Another form of opposition is based on the psychic costs of change. It is difficult for most of us to alter our methods of behavior. Also, the costs and benefits of the accepted structure are known. Should we decide to initiate a change, it may fail, causing us substantial embarrassment and loss of status. Consequently, precedent defines a safe path and there the incentives are much stronger to act "warily than daringly."

Inability to Change

An inability to change may be the result of conditions operating inside people, acting as mental blinders to thinking or behavior. Other obstacles originate within the organization—regardless of individual pliability.

Regularities of behavior essential to orderly life in organizations are programmed into members by indoctrination, training, imitation, or absorption of the organizational climate. Through these processes people are screened, groomed, fitted into, and weeded out of the ongoing system so that they possess the "proper" skills, attitudes, and personality traits. As a result individuals develop tunnel vision, programmed behaviors, and common values. Since they have become conditioned to a "way of life," the whole system becomes second nature to organizational members, and any change is seen as highly disruptive and threatening.

Barriers to change may be built into the organization itself. Limitations may be imposed by inadequacies in natural resources (e.g., raw material, location, etc.) or social constraints (e.g., competition, legislation, etc.). Other resources may be sunk costs, thus they are not convertible into some other form which would allow for adjustment to changing conditions. Obsolescence eventually afflicts most apparatus, knowledge, and skills.

Another reason it is difficult to change organizational structures or behaviors is because of their enmeshment in public laws, regulations, and adjudication, or in the organizations' own official rules and decisions. Constraints may be imposed by informal groupings and customary practice, which are not officially recognized but are just as binding and harder to detect and alter.

Finally, interorganizational agreements, such as labor contracts, impose limitations on organizational change. Plans may be upset by arrangements with suppliers, commitments to customers, promises to contractors, or pledges to public authorities. Very few organizations are able to escape the constraining effects of such interorganizational agreements.

STAGES OF ORGANIZATIONAL GROWTH AND DEVELOPMENT

"Like people and plants, organizations have a life cycle. They have a green and supple youth, a time of flourishing strength, and a gnarled old age... An organization may go from youth to old age in two or three decades, or it may last for centuries"—John Gardner (1967).

As organizations grow in size they tend to undergo a series of developmental changes. These changes include increases in volume and resources, changes in structure and interaction patterns, and changes in climate and objectives. Most organizations go through these stages from creation to maturity, although their rate of development may vary.

Key Forces in Organizational Development

The rate of development may vary greatly depending on changing forces in the external or internal environment. From an analysis of recent studies, Larry Griener (1972) found five key dimensions which determine the rate and elaboration of organizational development—the *age* and *size* of the organization, the stages of *evolution* and *revolution*, and the *growth rate* of the field. Each dimension influences the others over time and their interaction determines how an organization develops as it grows.

Age The same practices and structures are not maintained over an organization's life span. There are organizational and managerial problems that develop with time. Primary concerns for new emerging organizations are different from those of established ones. Behavior becomes more predictable in established organizations but difficult to change when needed.

Size An organization's problems and alternatives change dramatically as the volume of activity and number of personnel increase. With increasing size comes problems of coordination and communication, new functions and levels of hierarchy emerge, and jobs become more related.

Stages of evolution Evolution refers to periods of growth where no major disruptions occur in organizational structure or behavior. During these quieter periods only minor changes in organization patterns are necessary to maintain an acceptable growth rate.

Stages of revolution Revolution refers to periods of turbulence where substantial changes in organizational practices occur. Old practices and structures are no longer adequate and new ways of relating must be developed if the organization is to continue to grow or even to survive.

Growth rate The growth rate of the market environment of an organization influences the speed and urgency of the phases of evolution and revolution. Organizations with a rapidly expanding demand for its services, for example, will have to add employees and develop new structures faster than organizations with more stable environments.

Phases of Evolution and Revolution

There are five specific phases of evolution and revolution that a developing organization encounters. Each phase is both the result of an earlier phase and the cause of the following phase. Organizations with a growing demand for their services experience these phases more rapidly, but the propensity is to complete all five phases. These phases are illustrated in Fig. 3.1.

Phase 1: Creativity versus administration The overriding concern in new organizations is on creating and marketing products or services. Entrepreneurs enjoy frequent and informal communication with their employees, promising ownership benefits for long hours worked, and controlling activities in accordance to immediate market feedback.

As the firm grows, these informal administrative devices and the intense dedication exhibited by the original employers are no longer adequate, and the "leadership" crisis develops. A strong manager with administrative competence is needed to lead the company out of the prevailing chaos.

Phase 2: Direction versus autonomy Assuming that the organization will be able to obtain a competent administrator, it will probably embark on a period of sustained growth. The administrator will specialize jobs, divide activities into functional groupings, set up accounting systems and budgets, and formalize the communication structure.

Although this locus of responsibility and control is necessary to give the organization direction, the creative specialists and lower-level managers begin to realize that they are becoming restricted by this centralized hierarchy. Consequently, demands for increased "autonomy" are voiced. Unable to let go of their centralized administration, many organizations encounter increased turnovers and hostility, leading to threats of failure unless a more decentralized system can be established.

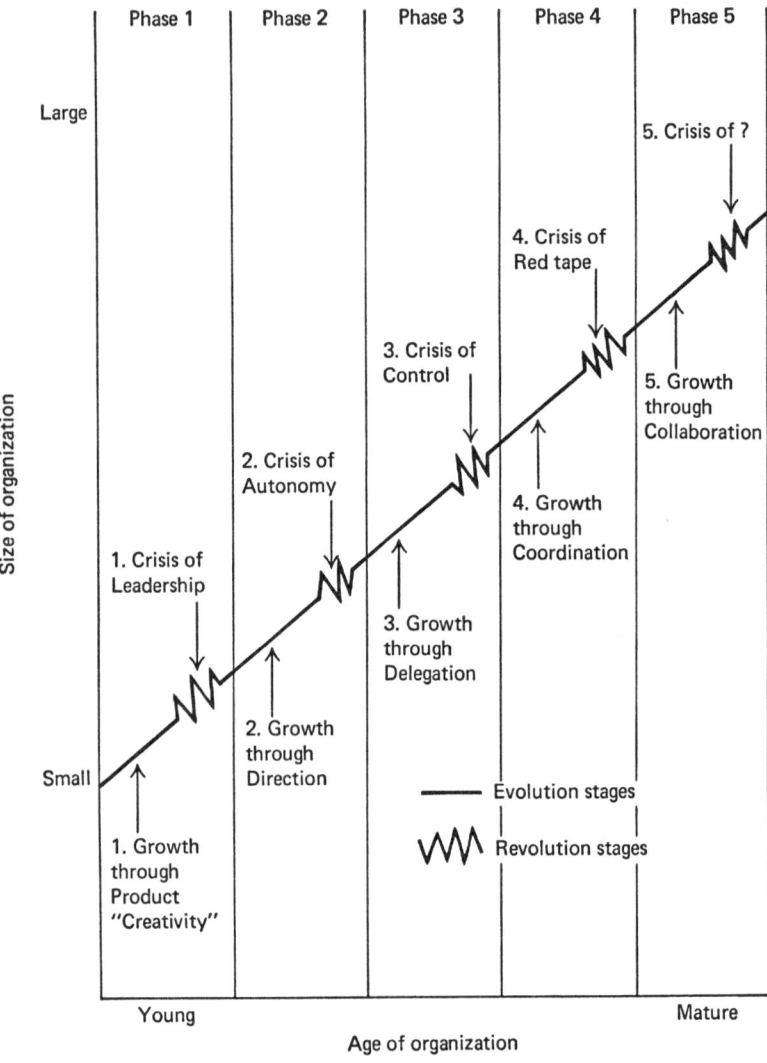

Phase 3: Delegation versus control Organizations entering into the next growth phase are able to delegate responsibility and establish a decentralized organizational structure, which gives greater responsibilities to lower-level managers, motivates employees

through subunit identification, and leaves them relatively autonomous from the central administration. The problem which arises from this management by exception is a lack of overall coordination of the autonomous subsystems because of central administration's abdication of control. Once the subunit managers have tasted autonomy, efforts to regain central control are usually futile and special integrating techniques must be developed.

Phase 4: Coordination versus red tape The increased coordination is achieved by applying additional centralized control systems. Decentralized subunits are merged into product groups, formal planning procedures are implemented, new staff members are hired to apply company-wide review programs, capital expenditures are judiciously awarded, and company-wide profit sharing is initiated. Consequently, subunit managers learn to justify their decisions with respect to the total organization and still retain decision-making responsibility.

Unfortunately the proliferation of control systems eventually exceeds their usefulness. The "red-tape" crisis develops when an unmanageable-paper system and innovation-killing systems are created and where procedures take precedence over problem-solving.

Phase 5: Collaboration versus over-involvement To overcome the alienation created by the bureaucratic-control system, strong interpersonal collaboration emerges and managers attempt to become more spontaneous, to solve their problems through interpersonal confrontations, and to utilize self-discipline. Cross-functional teams are established with staff support to solve specific problems; formal systems are simplified and conferences are increased; and educational programs are established to increase interpersonal and problem-solving skills.

Although many large organizations have now reached this stage of growth and development, probably none have yet completed it. Crises are already developing, centering around psychological and emotional fatigue and developing from the intensity of the interpersonal confrontations and emphasis on innovative teamwork. Preliminary solutions are also appearing, including employee sabbaticals, more flexible working hours, and the four-day work week.

If the organization is to continue to grow and develop, there must be a high level of awareness regarding the consequences of any planned change on the following revolution and how it will affect the overall organizational climate. The organization's values and image are important variables which limit the viability of some alternatives while enhancing the potency of others.

ORGANIZATIONAL CLIMATE

Organizational-development theorists attest that as an organization grows it must change its climate as well as its structure if it wishes to remain effective. Climate is a major force which influences behavior on the job. Organizational climate includes factors such as attitudes, expectations, cultural norms, and leadership styles which have potential behavioral consequences because they affect morale, satisfaction, emotional identification, achievement arousal, optimism, and other motivational variables.

An article in the *Harvard Business Review* by Harrison (1972) reveals that much of the conflict surrounding organizational change is really an ideological struggle. Organizational ideologies, or systems of thought, are the major determinants of organizational climate. These ideologies directly affect the organization through the behavior of its members and its ability to meet internal and external demands. They indirectly effect the organizational climate, which determines appropriate goals and values, relationships, expectations, control mechanisms, and communication styles. Understanding organizational ideologies and climate will provide the answers to questions such as: How are success and worth assessed? What can be expected by the organization from its members, and conversely? Are members expected to compete or cooperate, to be open or secretive, to be self-directed or follow orders? What kinds of control are legitimate or illegitimate?

Organizational climates are usually centered around one of four common ideologies: (1) power orientation, (2) role orientation, (3) task orientation, and (4) person orientation. Although seldom found as pure types, most organizational climates reflect a predominant orientation.

Power-oriented organizations are unwilling to be controlled by external laws or authorities. Laws and agreements are broken if they are inhibiting and the organization strives to dominate its environment regardless of the expense to others. Organizations, contracts, and even people are bought and sold without regard to human values or the general welfare.

Within the organization a similar "dog-eat-dog" atmosphere prevails as people struggle with their peers for personal advantages. It is only in older established firms that the power orientation is submerged in benevolent autocratic management, and old and loyal employees are cared for rather than exploited. As long as things go along smoothly the "velvet glove" will remain, but once a challenge is felt, the "iron fist" will again appear.

Role orientation develops as a defensive reaction to power orientation. The emphasis of this ideology is on orderliness and rationality. The preoccupations are with legitimacy, legality, and responsibility. Rights and privileges are well-defined and adhered to via agreements, rules, and procedures. Predictability of behavior, stability, and respectability are valued as much as competence, and the "correct" response is value as much as the most effective one.

In changing or competitive environments, role-oriented organizations would probably lack the flexibility and innovativeness to survive. Civil service, public utilities, or nonprofit organizations, on the other hand, can better endure the red tape because of their legally regulated and monopolistic environments.

In *task-oriented* organizations, achievement of a superordinate goal is the highest value and members, structures, and procedures are evaluated on this basis. Nothing, or no one, is permitted to get in the way of accomplishing the task. Consequently, personal needs and social considerations that are irrelevant to "getting the job done" are suppressed. Organizational structure is shaped and changed to meet task requirements and collaboration is sought on the basis of mutual goals.

Task orientation is most often found in small organizations whose members have come together because of a joint commitment or goal. Large organizations, operating in highly complex and changing environments, also exhibit this orientation in the form of "project teams" and "task forces." Because of internal conflicts and external stresses, task-oriented organizations often convert, after short periods of time, to role or power orientations.

People-oriented organizations exist primarily to serve the needs of their members and to provide a vehicle for the members to "do their own thing." The use of authority is minimal and individuals are expected to influence each other through relating, helping, and caring. Decisions are based on consensus and roles are assigned by personal preference. The goal is to allow all members to do enjoyable and meaningful work.

Examples of people-orientation may be found in groups of professionals such as engineers, consultants, psychologists, or doctors. There are increasing pressures on modern organizations to become more people-oriented. Highly educated young professionals are demanding meaningful work, and opportunities to learn and grow are often more important than organizational advancement.

Organizational Climate, Evolution, and Revolution

As an organization grows, its operating environment becomes more complex. To meet these changing demands, the internal decision-making and information-processing structures of the organization, as well as its ideologies and climate, must adjust. Depending upon its stage of development, different ideologies are required to allow the organization to progress through the revolution or evolution it is facing. Figure 3.2 illustrates how the stages of evolution and revolution match climate orientations to enable effective adaptation.

Growth phase	Climate orientation			
	Task	Power	Role	Person
Creativity	X			
Direction		X		
Delegation/ coordination			X	
Collaboration				X

Fig. 3.2. Climate orientation and stages of growth.

Creativity and Task Orientation

When an organization is in the birth stage, physical and mental energies are absorbed in making and marketing the product. Communication, feedback, and reactions are immediately and solely related to the task. Individuals' behavior and the organization's structure are evaluated under the task orientation. Authority is based on competence and members have shared values and goals.

At this stage, power orientation would interfere with the need to "get the task off the ground" and established. Role orientations are too inflexible for the rapid adjustment and multiple needs that exist at this stage. Finally, personal orientation cannot yet be afforded because all energies must be devoted to the superordinate organizational goal. Since organizational members share the organizational goal at this stage (or else they wouldn't be there), a high degree of personal satisfaction is obtained from moving the organization forward. "Doing the organization's thing" is equivalent to "doing your own thing." Later, when the organization is better established, individuals can branch out to pursue different areas of growth.

Direction and Power Orientation

During the direction-of-growth phase, formal budgeting, merit, and communication systems are established under the leadership of a manager who is responsible for instituting direction. Lower-level supervisors find themselves restricted and treated as functional specialists rather than autonomous decision-makers. As a result they feel torn between following orders and giving up responsibility, and regaining some initiative for themselves.

The climate is thus set for a shift to power orientation with a few aggressive people at the top policing those below and relying on reward and punishment to suppress covert rebellion. Since the controlling managers do not provide for the utilization of internal commitment, initiative, or independent judgment on the part of other organization members, they feel exploited, powerless, insecure, and deprived. As members become increasingly dissatisfied and leave the organization, top management begins to solve the crisis of autonomy through delegation.

Delegation—Coordination and Role Orientation

In the delegation phase, autonomy is restored by decentralizing and returning decision responsibility to subunits. In order to avoid losing control over these relatively independent subsystems, formal systems for achieving coordination are created in the following phase. Formal planning, job descriptions, and control systems are implemented by new staff personnel using elaborate procedures and paper processing systems. The ideology that best supports the striving for rationality, legitimacy, predictability, and responsibility is role orientation.

The perpetuation of rigid roles and reporting relationships, however, is insufficiently flexible to easily adapt to external changes and too narrow to accommodate individual need satisfaction. Consequently, although internal security and predictability are apparently achieved, opportunities for meeting higher level individual needs and the flexibility to rapidly adjust to changing environmental demands is absent.

Collaboration and Person Orientation

In the collaboration stage, strong interpersonal relationships are emphasized in an attempt to overcome the impersonality and inflexibility of the bureaucracy created in the delegation and coordination phases. People-orientation, where individuals are expected to influence each other through helpfulness, caring, and competence, provides the most supportive climate under this ideology. Consensus methods of decision-making and role assignment based on personal needs for growth are consistent with emphasis on across-function teams, the encouragement of new practices, and educational programs designed to train managers in conflict resolution and teamwork.

This type of climate-structure combination is well adapted to deal with complexity and change, as well as to provide opportunities for individual-need satisfaction. Matrix-type structures assemble the right teams for the appropriate problems. The rapid and rational assignment of people is accompanied by a high concern for one another's welfare, high motivation to obtain shared goals, and high satisfaction derived from meaningful and interesting work.

Organizational climates develop with the stages of organization growth. The congruence of ideology and structure affect organizational effectiveness in the way the roles are assigned, decisions are made, and the external environment is responded to. Even when they are congruent, however, organizational structures and ideologies are only internally viable when they match up with the needs, wants, and values of people within the system.

EFFECTS OF CLIMATE AND STRUCTURE ON ORGANIZATIONAL MEMBERS

Each of the climate-structure combinations discussed meets the needs of the organization and its members differently. A small organization, operating in the creativity stage, for example, needs task- or person-orientation to meet its members' needs for growth and autonomy and the task requirements of a changing environment. However, a large established organization, operating in a stable environment might find that role-orientation would better accommodate the stable and security-seeking people who are members. The climate-structure combination that is best for you as an individual depends on your own personal needs and values.

Occupational Values of Organizational Members

Carkhuff and Friel (1974) divide personal values in organizations into the dimensions of the physical, emotional, and intellectual.

Physical values involve the things you do physically or that have a physical effect on you. Role requirements and working conditions are examples of the things that determine physical values. Other examples are activity level, comfort, and rapidity of work.

Emotional values involve attitudes you feel about yourself and others. This is the affective or feeling dimension in the organization. Examples are satisfaction, challenge, pressure, trust, and responsibility.

Intellectual values involve the things that you think or know, or that affect your intellectual functioning. This is the cognitive or information-processing dimension. Examples of intellectual values are learning, creativity, communication, and planning.

To achieve maximum effectiveness in meeting both individual and organizational objectives, it is important that the desired content and level of individual values match the predominate type and level of ideological orientation in the organization. Often, however, a basic conflict exists between the climate and structure of the organization and the predominate values of individual members.

People have three primary concerns, which are most often the subject of ideological conflict:

1 Security against economic, political, or psychological deprivation.
2 Opportunity to commit efforts to goals and tasks that are personally meaningful.
3 Ability to pursue personal growth and development.

Security interests relate directly to all three of Carkhuff's and Friel's values. People desire to protect, maintain, and enhance the things that are physically, emotionally, and intellectually satisfying to them. Meaningful goals and tasks relate directly to important

Job concerns	Occupational values		
	Physical	Emotional	Intellectual
Security	Health Money Comfort Working conditions	Equality Trust Stability Caring	Independence Communication Rationality Understanding
Task relevance	Body condition Privacy Attractiveness Activity	Responsibility Commitment Involvement Compassion	Accomplishment Decision-making Planning Completion
Personal growth	Strength Prosperity Vacation Travel	Prestige Love Openness Intimacy	Learning Wisdom Creativity Perfection

Fig. 3.3. Relationships between organization members' occupational values and job concerns.

emotional and intellectual values concerning content, and to physical values relating to process. Finally, pursuit of personal growth may relate to physical, emotional, or intellectual dimensions. Figure 3.3 demonstrates how some of the important occupational values described in Chapter 2 relate to our primary job concerns.

Matching Individual and Organizational Values

For most organizations there is no perfect fit between personal values and organizational ideologies. As seen in Fig. 3.4, however, the task and person orientations appear to offer more opportunities to satisfy all three personal value categories than do the power and role orientations. Person-value organizational-ideology matches and mismatches at each stage of development will be described below with application to the case histories presented earlier.

Growth stage	Personal occupational values			Climate orientation
	Physical	Emotional	Intellectual	
Creativity	High: activity money prosperity	High: commitment involvement openness	High: communication creativity accomplishment	Task
Direction	Low: comfort strength privacy	Low: trust equality intimacy	Low: decision-making independence understanding	Power
Delegation/ coordination	Low: activity prosperity privacy	Low: compassion equality intimacy	Low: creativity planning wisdom	Role
Collaboration	High: strength activity vacation	High: involvement openness caring	High: communication understanding planning	Person

Fig. 3.4. Organizational stage of development, organizational ideology, and personal occupational values.

Creativity-task Stage

Organizations that promote frequent and informal communication, expect long hours of work, value creativity and achievement, and collaborate on the basis of mutual goals, offer abundant opportunities for, and often require, high physical activity, high emotional commitments, and high intellectual application and development. Salary generally matches heavy time commitment, high frequency of interpersonal communication, and superordinate goal commitment; it is the basis for a strong emotional commitment and precipitates the immediate responses necessary in a changing environment where there are demands for rapid information processing and creativity.

If you possess the high energy and achievement values described in Fig. 3.4, the creativity/task organization would be satisfying for you. If, however, your personal values do not meet the requirements, then you may find yourself very unhappy. The "match" is the key in all these situations. The negative consequences which follow for both the individual and the organization if a "mismatch" occurs are exemplified as in the case of Dick Larson.

Lakeside Laboratories possessed many of the ideologies and characteristics of the creativity/task organization. In fact, creativity and achievement were valued above all else. When Dick encountered Fred—a perceived competitor with higher values for activity, commitment, and accomplishment—he felt that he was losing control, self-respect, and commitment to his job. Because Dick lacked the necessary values of openness and communication, he never mentioned his discomfort to anyone, deciding instead to withdraw. Had he discussed his feelings with Mr. Halberson, the confusion could probably have been cleared up to the satisfaction of all involved.

Direction-power Stage

Formal, impersonal hierarchies, where only a few key managers take the responsibility for making decisions and establishing structure, leave other organizational members feeling restricted and apathetic, dissatisfied and anxious to "get even," or attempting to regain at least enough power to protect themselves and have some

Effects of Climate and Structure on Organizational Members 59

autonomy. Consequently, those with high physical-energy levels become competitive and seek to expand their control at the expense of others.

Where the "law of the jungle" prevails, it is difficult to feel secure in your job, or to be committed, intimate, or responsible to fellow employees. It also does not pay to be creative, unless the learning and strategies that you develop can be used against those seeking to discredit you.

Joe Brennon was confronted with a similar situation, where, in spite of his demonstrated competence and contribution, he was not given a deserved promotion because he did not conform to the social values of the power elite. He learned the hard way that it does not pay to ignore the "law of the jungle" in a direction/power-overted organization. A better fit would be obtained for Joe if he joined a creative or collaborative-oriented organization, where creativity, openness, and understanding were important.

Delegation/Coordination-role Stage

Individual value orientations are unlikely to be congruous with organizational ideologies at this stage for the following reasons. Bureaucratic structures rigidly define physical and intellectual activities, and impersonalization denies opportunities for emotional expression. Instead of being thwarted by personal power, as in the previous stage, individuals in this type of setting find all three value categories thwarted by rules and rigid structures.

This is a situation similar to the one Jean Lawrence found herself in at SOK Electronics. Although her position as Market Research Manager provided security, status, and monetary reward, it did not offer the independence, creativity, and emotional expression that her future as an interior designer promised. Her goal of setting up her own business would provide a creativity-task organization more in line with her personal values.

Collaboration-person Stage

Since this type of organization is primarily oriented toward developing its members potential and allowing its members to apply their talents to meaningful organizational tasks, it provides abundant opportunities for contributions to physical, intellectual, and emotional values.

A work environment where all are satisfied is sought with opportunities for people to be active in ways they prefer. A high emotional commitment is expected from those involved in project teams and in committee decision-making. Finally, individuals' intellectual interests are considered in educational offerings and in the rewards promised for innovations.

Ideally, most family organizations should be established to aid their members in developing their potentials along the lines of collaborative/person-oriented models. If for some reason all the members do not share in equal opportunities to participate, the organization can shift to either power-orientation or role-orientation, as in the case of Ron and Janet Samuels.

Their relationship began when they were in college, aiding each other's personal development with mutual concern and collaboration. The circumstances associated with their family development led to a role-oriented organization, which favored Ron's continued personal development and sacrificed Janet's opportunities for personal growth. As the couple gradually developed different values, their organization and their relationship began to deteriorate. It even took on some characteristics of direction-power orientation when Ron "suggested" that Janet change in a manner he prescribed to become more like him. Although Ron has considered "quitting" the organization, another more fruitful possibility would be to reestablish a collaborative/person-oriented organization, where Janet could pursue her own unique potentials in a manner best suited for her.

Implications for Organizational Members

In order for an organization to survive (which is definitely in the interests of its employees), it must continually protect, maintain, and enhance the values and structural qualities that advance its interests. It must be concerned with (1) an effective response to complex environments, (2) responding readily to change, and (3) integrating internal efforts towards organizational needs and goals.

This sometimes includes the subordination of individual values and needs to those of the organization. Unfortunately, for most organizations there is no perfect fit of structure and climate with individual needs and values. A mixture of these things and their consequences will almost always result in conflict for both the organization and its members.

For most individuals, however, organizations at the creativity or collaboration stage, with task or people orientations, offer the best potential for congruency with personal needs and values. This implies that organizations which offer the best advantages are either small and new or large and well-established. Smaller and newer organizations inevitably become larger and older (if they continue to exist); thus a collaborative and person-oriented organization would be the optimal choice.

But what about individuals in organizations of intermediate size and development? In these organizations, power and control by other individuals or by rules inhibit individual expression. Harrison (1972) suggests that we learn to create and maintain diverse ideologies and structures to provide for the expression of individual differences in values and needs. This means that organizations may have to be composed of separate parts—ideologically and structurally homogeneous between individuals and environments, but quite different from one another.

This climate and structure mix would result in conflicting, but mutually interdependent, subsystems, which would considerably increase internal conflict. However, these subsystems would be very effective in dealing with changing and complex environments and in maximizing satisfactions for different types of people.

Chapter 4

The Personal Development Strategy:
A Systematic Process for Personal and Organizational Development

Up to this point we have helped you explore the process of development and change in both individuals and in organizations. You noted that behavioral scientists have studied the *commonalities* of change in the process of development for both individuals and organizations. In other words, behavioral scientists have studied large numbers of cases and have summarized their findings in *normative* terms—that is, their findings describe the "average" person or organization. But we know that people and organizations are unique, and that sometimes theories do not fully explain all cases.

For example, Sheehy (1976) describes seven stages of adult development. Yet, it is possible that you may know one or more people who have not progressed through these stages in the timeframes or order that these scientists suggest. By design, normative theories or explanations attempt to partition and eliminate uniqueness in individuals and, instead, stress commonalities. Normative explanations can be very helpful when you want to compare yourself or your organization to some criterion or average or norm. But when you are more concerned with comparing individuals with themselves or emphasizing their differences or uniqueness with regard to some norm, you are talking in *idiographic* or personalistic terms.

Earlier we observed that two people who have almost the same background, training, education, and job description—in a normative sense—can have completely different reactions to their jobs.

One may be very dissatisfied with his or her work, peers, and prospects for the future, while the other person is quite content. An idiographic or personalized study of these two individuals could explain these differences. It is our view that knowing both the normative *and* the idiographic explanations is necessary for a total picture of the person and the organization.

We hope to reinforce this point several times throughout this book, because it has been our observation that programs, advice, and decisions that have been based on one or the other of these explanations have been the source of a great deal of dissatisfaction in both workers and those who study these workers. Most of the remainder of this book will deal with strategies and techniques for increasing your *personalized* understanding of yourself, your organization, and the satisfactions and dissatisfactions you experience therein.

CHANGE VS. PLANNED CHANGE VS. PERSONALIZED CHANGE

It is a truism to say that change is everywhere, and that simply being a human being connotes change. Whether we like it or not we are constantly changing. The most obvious change is that of physical maturity. But our attitudes and values also constantly change, albeit at different rates and to different degrees.

Oftentimes people are heard to say that the organizations they are with haven't changed a bit in the last 30 years. Unfortunately, these individuals are mistaken. You saw in Chapter 3 that organizations do indeed change and develop, almost constantly. You may be familiar with Alvin Toffler's (1970) book, *Future Shock*, which describes the dizzying rate of change that all of us must face daily and what the psychological effects that this steady diet of what appears to be unbridled change can do to us.

We want to contrast change with what is called "planned change." *Change* is often characterized by movement, randomness, directionlessness, and unconnectedness. *Planned change*, on the other hand, is conscious, directed, and strives to integrate the past with the future in some meaningful way. Organizational-development specialists and futurists focus most of their energy on the planned change. Planned change is evident in communities where good architectural planning retains the character and harmony of the past, while integrating innovation so that a "fit" is evident. This can be contrasted with the gaudy, unplanned, and "misplaced" look of much of our urban development.

The difference between planned and unplanned change is evident on a personal level. The man or woman who moves from job to job every 6 to 18 months, from the same problem situation in one job to a similar problem situation in the next job, is one example. Job-hoppers often do not know themselves or their needs and values, nor have they taught themselves to be observant of their work environment and its demands and payoffs. Contrast these individuals with individuals who terminated their employment or have it terminated, and who invest their time and effort in exploring their own needs and values, evaluate their difficulties with their former employer, and then look for a position that will better mesh with their needs.

What we want to do is help you become proficient in planning change. In fact we want to help you develop a strategy for "personalized" planned change that goes beyond the normative strategies and techniques the organizational-development people routinely use to plan and manage change. We want to help you develop a Personal Development Strategy.

WHY A PERSONAL DEVELOPMENT STRATEGY?

Each of us is constantly beset by potential crises and dissatisfactions, which are manifestations of change in our lives. But how we meet these crises and dissatisfactions is very important in determining how much we are able to grow and develop our potential. To deal effectively and successfully with change, we need a game plan, which will give us direction and enough flexibility to achieve a better understanding of the normal changes that take place in our psychological growth during the course of adulthood. And we need to develop the necessary skills that will make it possible to operationalize or use this understanding. At any point in time, an effective game plan, or what we prefer to call a *Personal Development Strategy*, can help you to reevaluate and restructure your life so that you can take full advantage of your potential to self-actualize and achieve the satisfaction and fulfillment you seek in both your personal and professional life. This book is designed to help you use this Personal Development Strategy.

A DESCRIPTION OF THE PERSONAL DEVELOPMENT STRATEGY

A Personal Development Strategy is a method or process of personalized, planned change that has been modified from the Contact Counseling Model developed by Len Sperry (1975) in *Developing Skills in Contact Counseling*.

Contact Counseling is a problem-solving/problem-preventing set of skills, where psychological "contact" is the theme and climate. When two people are communicating, "contact" is present if one or both parties is able to psychologically touch the core of the other person's being, usually by getting and staying in the other person's frame of reference. Contact Counseling is not something mysterious, ethereal, or difficult to learn. It is similar to psychotherapy and organizational development, and yet it is neither. Rather it is a type of communication in which one person (the counselor) helps another person (the counselee) to think about and answer six life-coping questions. In this way, the counselee can come to think, feel, and act in an healthier and more productive way.

Contact Counseling can also be thought of as a self-counseling technique, in which a person gets in closer "contact" with self to problem-solve/problem-prevent. The six life-coping questions the counselee is helped to deal with are the following:

1 What is my problem or *situation?*
2 How does it make me *feel* and *act?*
3 What does it *mean* to me?
4 *What* can I *do* about it?
5 *Will I* do it?
6 *How* will I *achieve* it?

The Contact Counseling process works like this: The counselor helps the counselee to assess his or her situation (1) and reaction to it (2), which reflect the counselee's frame of reference and Personality Style (3). In order to help the counselee know that he or she is understood and to understand and accept self in spite of his or her difficulties, the counselor responds to the counselee. In a sense, the counselor holds up a mirror for the counselee to see the real meaning of his or her behavior, its consequences, and its basic goals and values. As the real problem is defined, a new goal—which is the exact opposite of the old goal—is set. Goal setting (4), commitment to the new goal (5), and the particular approaches to achieving the goal (6) make up the guiding or motivating phase of the counseling process.

This process is simple and straightforward. The counselor's role is to serve as coach and teammate—encouraging, reflecting, confronting, and facilitating the counselee's inquiry during the questioning process. This approach has been taught to persons at all levels of management, as well as to professional and paraprofessionals who help professionals with excellent results.

The Personal Development Strategy is a modification of the six life-question steps of Contact Counseling. The six stages of the Personal Development Strategy are as follows:

1 Situation and Organization Assessment
2 Personal Assessment
3 Assessment of Person—Organization Match-mismatch
4 Decision-making
5 Commitment
6 Implementation and Evaluation

The rest of this chapter will be devoted to describing each of these stages and overviewing the rest of the book.

Situation and Organization Assessment

Perhaps it would be helpful to present a model for understanding a person's behavior in the context of an organization. Figure 4.1 presents such a model.

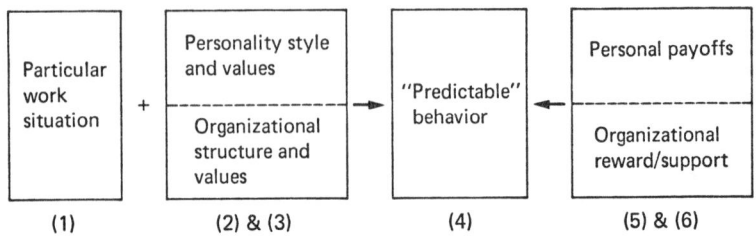

Fig. 4.1. The context for individual behavior in an organization.

In this model, an individual's behavior can be understood or explained as being a function of his or her own values and personality, and also as being influenced by the organization and the particular situation in which the person is involved. The individual's personality style and values (2) are constantly interacting with the organizational structure and value dynamics (3). This interacting may be a smooth meshing of both systems or one that is a poor "fit." In any case, the internal (thoughts, attitudes, feelings) and external (actions, words) behavior (4) that result from (1), (2), and (3) are most often reinforced in terms of personal payoffs (5), which may be positive or negative, as well as of short or long term, in terms of the organization's reward, support, and maintenance systems (6). Personal-payoff and organizational-payoff systems will be described in later chapters.

Stage (1) of the Personal Development Strategy involves an assessment of (1), (3), and (6), the work situation, and the organization's values and payoff system. You will want to explore the nature of your problem and the dissatisfaction that results from it.

In terms of the organization, you will want to assess what it expects and demands of its members in terms of rules, regulations, and policies, whether written or unwritten; what it enforces and doesn't enforce; what it's stage of development is; what internal and external demands affect its functioning; what the resultant work climate is; what its reward and support systems are; and what type of management/communication styles, as well as interpersonal relationships, are encouraged.

In terms of the situation, you will want to find and analyze the particular circumstances, the particular people involved, and whatever other factors might be involved in the problem and dissatisfaction you are experiencing. A major goal of this assessment should be to focus on the source of the problem and to establish whether the problem stems from your own personality needs, the demands and expectations of the organization, or some other situational factors. Chapter 6 focuses on techniques for assessing (1), (3), and (6).

Personal Assessment

Personal assessment is concerned with your personality style and needs and values (2) as well as your personal payoffs (6). In addition, you will also learn about your "predictable" patterns of behaving and reacting (4). You will need to explore your own level of personal development and your value system in terms of physical, emotional, and intellectual value indicators. Keying in on your own values will give you a number of clues to your personality style which will be invaluable to you in charting specific ways to self-actualize your potentials and talents. Chapter 5 will focus on teaching you to assess your personal needs, values, and payoff systems, and will give you some further techniques for understanding your behavior.

Assessment of Person/Organization Match-mismatch

As you increase your understanding of your situation, your organization, and your personality, it becomes increasingly important to integrate these oftentimes disparate pieces of information. As you proceed a pattern, which will suggest the "degree of fit" between you and your organization, should emerge. This pattern will confirm many of your conjectures about why you have been rebuked for certain things and rewarded for others; why have you been unnoticed at times and the recipient of "unexpected" praise or punishment at others, or whatever. At this point, you will be able to quantify your perceptions and data in a useful measure, called the *Match-mismatch Index*, which is described in detail in Chapter 7.

Decision-making

After discerning the nature and source of the problem and dissatisfaction, it is now possible to move in the direction of possible problem solutions. The first step involves setting up a series of alternative courses of action that can resolve the problem. Then a decision as to the best course of action must be made. In Chapter 7 a comprehensive and systematic method for decision-making is presented. This approach simultaneously relates the information you have developed in stages (1), (2), and (3) to the alternative courses of action or options.

Commitment

It has been said that commitment is at the very core of constructive change, for it is of little value to engage in extensive personal and organizational assessment and decision-making without proceeding to a solution. It is not enough for you to say that you wish you could change. There is a very significant difference between what you *want* or would like to do, and what you actually *will* do. In other words, there is a difference between intentions and actions. Commitment is the name of the game—the change game!

It is crucial that you set deadlines and make a contract for change with yourself—or with another person if you don't feel you can "trust" yourself—whether it be verbal or in writing. You will need to consider how you can reorder your personal-payoff system so that your attempts to function in a different manner will be reinforced and so that you will not become discouraged and even further dissatisfied with your situation. Although no one chapter focuses on commitment, you will find a number of helpful hints about commitment in many of the following chapters.

Implementation and Evaluation

In the organizational-development literature, intervention strategies and techniques are staples. These strategies run the gamut from brainstorming to sensitivity training, and from setting up objectives or performance standards to dieting and exercise. A number of strategies and tactics for goal achievement in changing organizations will be described in Chapter 10. Whether a decision to change oneself, to stay in the organization without attempting self-change, or to change the organization is required, a number of self-development and survival skills can be found in Chapter 9. Whatever the decision may be and regardless of the nature of commitment, it is mandatory for you to be as objective and systematic at this stage of the process as you were at the beginning. Chapter 8 should provide you with further information and encouragement in following through on your new decided course of action. The five steps of the Implementation-Evaluation procedure will help you to achieve your desired change.

SELF-ACTUALIZATION AS A GOAL AND CRITERION FOR PERSONALIZED CHANGE

Our discussion so far has focused on the process of change. We have talked about how to achieve change, but now we need to talk about the purpose and direction of change. We need to consider our goal(s) for personal change. It is important that we be able to clearly specify these goals, because they have become our criterion or measures of the extent to which we have achieved them.

One of the most widely discussed criterion for self-development is self-actualization—a concept which has been called by various names. The most widely used name is the one coined by Abraham Maslow. Maslow and psychologists of a similar persuasion believe that there is an internal drive in a person to actualize his or her potentials; they labeled this drive *self-actualization*. Whether or not such a drive or motivation exists, it is clear from the number of articles and books, workshops, and courses devoted to this topic that self-actualization is an important concern for many people.

In *Toward a Psychology of Being,* Maslow (1968) characterized self-actualization as:

> ... an episode, or a spurt in which the powers of the person come together in a particularly efficient and intensely enjoyable way, and in which he is more integrated and less split, more open for experience, more idiosyncratic, more perfectly expressive or spontaneous, or fully functioning, more creative, more humorous, more ego-transcending, more independent of his lower needs, etc. He becomes in these episodes more truly himself, perfectly actualizing his potentialities, closer to the core of his being.

Maslow's model of self-actualization emerged from his study of present and historical persons who were judged to be very psychologically healthy. This clinical study suggested an index or set of criteria to those qualities associated with the psychologically healthy or actualized person. These qualities or characteristics are listed in *Toward a Psychology of Being* as:

1. Superior perception of reality
2. Increased acceptance of self, of others, and of nature
3. Increased spontaneity
4. Increased problem-solving ability
5. Increased autonomy, and resistance to enculturation
6. Increased detachment and desire for privacy
7. Greater freshness of appreciation, and richness of emotional reaction
8. Higher frequency of peak experiences
9. Changed (the clinician would say, improved) interpersonal relations
10. Increased identification with the human species
11. Greatly increased creativeness
12. More democratic character structure
13. Certain changes in the value system

Self-actualization consists primarily of being "time competent" and "autonomous" or inner-directed. Time competent refers to one's ability to tie the past and the future to the present in a meaningful continuity, while fully living in the present. As such, the more self-actualized person appears to be less burdened by resentment, guilts, and regrets from the past than is the less-actualized person. Autonomy or inner-direction refers to one's ability to be liberated from rigid adherence to parental or cultural values and to flexibly apply his personally formulated set of values and principles to deal effectively with problem situations.

Everett Shostrum, a humanistic psychologist, has developed the *Personal Orientation Inventory* to assess a person's self-actualizing tendencies. This paper and pencil questionnaire is comprised

of 150 forced-choice statements of value and behavior judgments believed to be related to such dimensions of self-actualization as time competence and inner-directed support. A number of other psychologists have developed similar models of the more fully human person, although none has been as well developed and supported by clinical evidence. Arthur Combs has described the Adequate Person; Hubert Bonner has written about the Proactive Person; and Carl R. Rogers has described the Fully Functioning Person. These descriptions basically dovetail with Maslow's description of the Self-actualizing Person.

CRITICISMS OF SELF-ACTUALIZATION AS A CRITERION FOR CHANGE

One of the main problems with Maslow's index or set of criteria is very few people can meet them. In fact, Maslow only came up with 49 people, present and historical, who personified these traits. Before he died, Maslow estimated that only about 1 percent of the total population was truly self-actualizing. And that can be very discouraging to some. It has been our experience that businessmen who have discussed Maslow's criteria inevitably conclude that such a person wouldn't last very long at their company. The ideal, self-actualized person, they say, seems too aloof, too much a loner, and too different in outlook from the average worker; he probably wouldn't be able to "fit" into the organization.

Later in his professional career, Maslow (1965) turned toward the world of work and wrote a book called *Eupsychian Management*. In it he described his psychological utopia, predicting from what he knew about self-actualizing people, what kind of culture would evolve if 1000 healthy families migrated to some deserted land where they could work out their own destiny.

Maslow's colleagues have published the results of experiments to put Maslow's self-actualizing principles into practice in business and industrial settings. Needless to say, the results were not very favorable or awe-inspiring. Probably the main reason for these disappointing findings is that individual employees and organizations have to be treated as unique entities. Self-actualization programs that put a high premium on worker self-direction and responsibility, when the workers aren't ready or willing to "develop" in this direction, are apparently doomed to failure from the start. These programs were actually counterindicated, as they were directly "opposed" to individual needs and values or the organization's support and reward system.

Another criticism of self-actualization as a goal of change has been made by Shostrum (1976) in his book, *Actualizing Therapy*. Shostrum makes a distinction between self-actualiz*ing* and self-actualiz*ation*. He defines *self-actualizing* as an active process of being and becoming increasingly inner-directed and integrated at the levels of thinking, feeling, and bodily response. *Self-actualization*, on the other hand, is a product or end-point. This distinction between process and product is crucial, according to Shostrum. Thus, whereas Maslow could predict that only 1 percent of the population was self-actualized, Shostrum predicts that about 50 percent of the population could be considered self-actualizing. Shostrum believes that actualizing is a process of moving from normal manipulation toward growth and the unfolding of human potentials. This growth occurs in all successful teaching, human-relations programs, and therapy. According to his research, at least one-half of the population has the potential to grow and develop in this manner. We find Shostrum's distinction to be both helpful and hope giving.

Viktor Frankl has leveled perhaps the most trenchant criticism at the self-actualization concept. Frankl, eminent psychiatrist and founder of the school of Logotherapy, reacts against the prevailing connotations of self-actualization, which are "happiness" and "doing your own thing." Frankl states that self-actualization is not man's ultimate destiny, nor is it his primary intention. Frankl believes that if self-actualization becomes one's goal or criterion, one contradicts the self-transcendent quality of human existence, itself. He states that, like happiness, self-actualization is a by-product of the fulfillment of meaning in a person's life. Furthermore, Frankl warns, if one sets out to actualize self rather than fulfill the basic meaning in his or her life, self-actualization immediately loses its justification.

For Frankl, actualization is the process of realizing or actualizing values or meanings in one's life. This process is basically self-transcendent rather than self-centered. Frankl believes that a person can only actualize his meaning by going beyond self, or transcending self. In his book, *Psychotherapy and Existentialism*, Frankl (1967) concludes "that a person finds self to the extent to which he or she loses self in the first place, be it for the sake of something or someone, for the sake of a cause or a fellowman, or 'for the sake of God'."

For persons like Frankl, "doing your own thing" can never be self-actualizing if "your thing" infringes on another's freedom or in any way lacks social responsibility. In short, the self-actualized person could not be considered a selfish person.

A growing number of social scientists have recognized the social interdependence that exists between individuals. Although they may not use the terminology of self-transcendence, they talk of mutual respect, cooperation, and intimacy, which are really synonyms of self-transcendence.

According to Frankl, the self-transcendent person experiences happiness as a by-product of his "going beyond himself," and other psychologists agree with this notion. Everett Shostrum states that self-actualizing cannot be equated with "fun" or "happiness." For Shostrum, self-actualizing involves a zest and challenge of adventure not ordinarily associated with the usual definitions of "happiness." Donald Campbell, past president of the American Psychological Association, agrees. He says that "the direct pursuit of happiness is a recipe for an unhappy life."

Morale is one clear indication of self-transcendence in an organization. The extent to which morale is high among a group of workers, to that extent will individual workers be working for the sake of someone or something else. This self-transcendent behavior clearly seems to be based on the "common good" rather than individual self-interest. Unmistakably, the individual worker's sense of happiness and satisfaction is the by-product or effect of the spirit of cooperation or morale, rather than the goal.

HOW WE DEFINE SELF-ACTUALIZATION

Our experience with people and organizations has lead us to a hearty acceptance of Frankl's view of self-actualization as the actualizing or realizing of meanings or values in a person's life, which by definition is a self-transcendent effort. Our experience has also confirmed the results of the Maslow experiments where self-actualizing principles were instituted as the goals of the organization. Like the Maslow researchers, we have observed that actualization is perceived differently by different workers, either because of their needs and values, or because of the organizational values and structures. We therefore find Maslow's unidimensional concept of self-actualization—with its 13 characteristic behavior—to be unapplicable to many personal and organizational situations. Rather, we conceive self-actualization to consist of movement in the Psychological Healthy/Synergy direction on the Personality Style/Value Continuum(s) that relates to the individual's needs and level of development. To put it another way, self-actualization, or the goal for planned personal change, is actually specified in the first four stages of the Personal Development Strategy.

A CONCLUDING NOTE

We have now come full circle. First we discussed planned and unplanned change and the need for a Personal Development Strategy. Then we described the six stages of planned personal change that make up the Personal Development Strategy. Next we discussed the purpose or goal direction of the planned change, which involved us in a number of descriptions and criticisms of the term self-actualization. We concluded by saying that we must personalize and operationalize self-actualization in terms of the first four stages of the Personal Development Strategy.

Chapter 5
Finding Out Where You're At

The disparity between organizational and individual goals is something most of us have faced. Because of the movement towards greater industrialization and urbanization in our society, we find that "making it" may mean coming to grips with an impersonal bureaucracy, loss of identity, and/or subordination of our needs to the organization's needs. The rapid process of change also has an impact on our personal lives. Social movements, such as the Women's Liberation movement, have had a profound impact on our family structure and have changed the traditional mode of family living. Our subordination to an organization and/or to the changing values of our society produces feelings of not having control over our lives, a sense of dissatisfaction with our careers, and/or a search for other avenues of personal fulfillment.

Faced with a conflict between our needs and the organization's needs, we often do not know what to do. Oftentimes, our lack of being able to select a course of action is because we are not aware of better alternatives. The O'Neills (1975), writing in *Shifting Gears*, state that the problem is often just the opposite. We are not able to make decisions because of a glut of alternatives. Confronted with a multitude of potential choices, we feel overwhelmed because we have no basis on which to assess which alternative is best suited to our needs, values, and goals.

In developing your *Personal Development Strategy*, it is crucial that you obtain an accurate assessment of your needs and values.

Using that information as a basis for selecting a course of action will greatly enhance the probability of that choice being correct. The first step in developing a plan of action is understanding your behavior. Chapter 2 explained how our behavior develops and changes. Now it is time to help you assess your behavior and determine your personal needs and values.

The following material is designed to assist you in learning about developmental tasks which are appropriate to your age group. Also, you will explore your value system in terms of physical, emotional, and intellectual value indicators. Identifying your personal values will give you several ideas about your personality style and will help you to plot specific ways of developing your potential and talents. Finally, you will identify your personality style, which will help you to understand your predictable pattern of behaving and reacting. Your personality style will help you to explain how you achieve your goals and will provide clues as to why you act the way you do and whether your behavior helps or hinders your goal achievement.

Before we begin helping you to develop your personal assessment, we need to discuss the importance of an accurate self-assessment. In order for you to construct an effective Personal Development Strategy, your self-assessment should be as accurate as possible. Your assessment is based upon where you think you are, as you see yourself through your own eyes. Your self-exploration is guided by how well you can observe your experiences and perceive the reactions of others around you. If you are open and attentive to the cues relevant to your experiences, your self-assessment will be highly accurate and reliable. However, you need to be aware of some of the shortcomings of self-assessment techniques so that you can guard against their jeopardizing the accuracy of your work. Even if we are willing, we still may not be able to describe ourselves accurately upon demand. Self-assessments are based on what we are willing or able to say when asked.

What we say about ourselves may or may not be what we truly feel. Even if we have the best of intentions, we may not be able to give an accurate description because other perceptions interfere and create a measure of distraction or distortion. What we say about ourselves is affected by what we are "supposed" to say. Also, some parts of our personality may not be assessed simply because they are so threatening that we cannot openly admit having them, even though they may be clearly apparent to others.

Despite such shortcomings, self-assessments are valuable. What you have to say about yourself and how you describe yourself will provide valuable information. Because of the symbolic nature of your self-assessment—i.e., how you describe your behavior and the uses you make of such behavior—it has a high value in assisting your understanding of how you behave. Employed as a description of your behavior, your self-assessment can provide you with valuable data about what is important to you.

It is our belief that while your self-assessment may not provide you with a "totally accurate" picture of yourself, it does provide you with some valuable information. To ensure the accuracy of your self-assessment, you need to keep in mind the following three important points:

1 Be as honest as you can. Do not try to respond as you would *like* to be, but respond the way you believe you *really* are. If necessary, complete the exercises in private and do not share your responses until you are ready.

2 Solicit other people's advice and reactions to your responses. If necessary, modify your responses accordingly.

3 Try to identify specific behavioral evidence to support your beliefs. Self-assessments are based on perceptions, or the way we think we are, and they need to be checked against an objective data base whenever possible.

WHERE TO BEGIN—AWARENESS

The starting point in any self-improvement plan is sensing that something is wrong, that things could be better, or that something else needs to be done. The case of Joe Brennon presents a good illustration of the starting point in trying to find out where you are —i.e., an awareness of a feeling of dissatisfaction.

For Joe, the demands of the University stifled his creativity by not letting him express his individuality. He felt that his style of dress and appearance were important in maintaining the image he had of himself. However, the demands made on him at the University were such that they actively pressured him to change to a more acceptable behavior pattern. Joe's marginal merit increases and not receiving the promotion effectively communicated the University faculty's position, that either he change or look elsewhere for a new position. Joe's reaction was manifested in physical symptoms, feelings of distress, and a decrease in productivity. However, Joe felt strongly that his need to express himself was important and necessary in order to sustain his identity. His family's needs added to his feelings of stress. Joe knew something had to change. He didn't know what to do or where to begin, but Joe was aware—intensely so—that all was not well.

Now, let us take a look at *your* current position. You are probably searching for answers and wondering what to do. Responses to a series of diagnostic questions will begin to help you to organize your thoughts and feelings and will give you the "lay of the land." In the space provided, try to answer each of the following questions as specifically as you can:

1 Are you aware of feelings of distress in your life?

Joe Brennon was upset with his situation and he knew it. Ron Samuels was embarrassed by his wife's lack of social and intellectual skills. Jean Lawrence was discontented with the nature of her work at SOK.

Dick Larson was unhappy on the inside with Fred Steggart, but tried to maintain an appearance of being satisfied.

When were you first aware that something was wrong? What was the situation? What did you do about it? Did it help? What are you aware of now? What is the situation? Be specific in your answers.

2 Do you desire a change in your life-problem situation?

Caught in a conflict situation, most of us want the other person and/or the organization to change. Changing our situation may mean that *we* have to change and that *we* are responsible for wanting the change.

Jean did not like her "Girl Friday" responsibilities at SOK. She was dissatisfied with the lack of responsibility and permanence this position provided. She liked her colleagues and the atmosphere at SOK but knew that she had to initiate a change to be happy.

When did you first experience a desire to change your situation? What precipitated your desire to change? What current situation do you want to change? How will you have to change? How will the organization have to change? Be specific in your answers.

3 Do you accept the emotional nature of your problem?

Most of the problems we deal with are caused by our "gut" reactions to the demands and expectations put upon us by our employers, spouses, friends, etc. We do not like what we are asked to do. The other person will not do what we want him or her to do. Thus we become upset and most often will not listen to logical explanations of the other side of the issue. We either withdraw, become revengeful, or pull a power-play if we have the authority.

Our thoughts, feelings, and attitudes need to be accepted and examined before constructive action can occur. Dick is a good example of what happens when you refuse to acknowledge your feelings of resentment and competition. He dealt with his problem by withdrawing.

What feelings do you have about your job problem? What effect do they have on your behavior? What do you want the other side to do that they are not doing? What precipitated your feelings? Be specific in your answers.

4 Do you accept the possibilities and limitations of potential change strategies?

When we investigate alternatives and their potential outcomes, there is no guarantee that any approach or choice will solve our problem. Each choice always seems to offer a certain amount of risk. On the other hand, the change strategy we select can have a positive "pay-off." Additional choices and alternatives are one of the "pay-offs."

Jean did not know what would happen if she decided to express her dissatisfaction to the Vice President. She was also aware of the bleak job market. In retrospect, the change strategies she followed produced results which she did not and probably could not have anticipated. Dick, on the other hand, seemed to accept withdrawal as the only strategy he could follow. In his case, about the only result was that he changed jobs. Nothing else changed.

What alternatives do you see yourself having? What are their potential limitations? What are their potential possibilities? Be specific in your responses.

5 Are you willing to voluntarily initiate action?

Each of us is responsible for our feelings and behavior. It is we who have feelings of distress, dissatisfaction, unhappiness, and discontentment. These are the feelings we want to change. No one can do it for us because it is our problem. We own them and can change them only by doing something about them.

Jean acted by speaking to the Vice President. Dick acted by leaving. Joe was beginning to realize that he had to do something soon if he was to avoid personal and family breakdowns. Ron could not maintain his marriage in its current state.

What is stopping you from taking action? Where do you want to start? When will you do it? What commitment will you make to taking action?

Awareness is the starting place—the catalyst that sparks movement. We may not know what we want, what has to be done, where to go, or where to start, but we do know when we are unhappy and dissatisfied. The diagnostic questions you just answered will help you to describe your current situation and your thoughts and feelings about that situation. You probably will not discover anything new. If anything, the questions may have induced further anxiety about your seemingly hopeless situation. However, it is important for you to become aware of "where you're at" and the discomfort you are feeling as a result of that seemingly hopeless situation.

Most of us find it difficult to move beyond the awareness stage. In response to feelings of dissatisfaction, a defensive reaction occurs. We try to protect ourselves by blaming others, by belittling ourselves and believing that we cannot do anything to change our supervisor or our job, or by criticizing those people who evaluate us. The defensive response has as its goal, justification of our old behavior. The process is one of blaming others and/or the organization for our feelings of being dissatisfied; and by shifting the responsibility for our unhappiness and inaction, we abdicate responsibility for our behavior.

Another response to being dissatisfied is denying the problem. Pushing the problem out of our conscious awareness does not change the situation—it results in our living a fraudulent life. We try to "look good" on the outside, but end up "feeling bad" on the inside.

A television commercial vividly presents the denial response. An attractive model, who is posing for a photograph, is asked how her love life is. She says, "Beautiful, wonderful, out-of-sight." She works hard to maintain the facade of happiness, but when pushed, she is capitulated into expressing her feelings of loneliness.

This commercial demonstrates how denial works. We build an image and establish behavior that is designed to enhance that image; but when put in a stress situation, inner feelings of dissatisfaction are manifested.

Defensive behavior and denial will not solve the problem, but they do ensure that nothing will be changed. The ironic thing is that we want the problem to be solved, yet our behavior suggests that we are actively seeking to maintain the current situation. We do, in fact, *resist* change!

When we work with the familiar, within a framework of accustomed behavior, we build a behavior pattern that is based on clear expectations. If we try to take action and change, we become more vulnerable, less sure of our position. No matter how uncomfortable the familiar is, fear of the unknown and fear of what *might* happen if we change are potent forces, which prevent us from changing.

In order for us to be responsive to an awareness of feelings of dissatisfaction and to initiate the next step, we must lower our protective mechanisms—that is, our protective mechanisms are no longer able to protect us. The status quo must be changed, either by coercion or by reducing the threat and resistance to change.

Joe was experiencing a demeaning process at the University—his identity was being humiliated and his professional growth was being stunted. All in all, he was pretty miserable. Thus the threat and resistance to change were reduced. In order for Joe to solve his feelings of distress, he would have to capitulate to the University's demands, try to change the University's reward structure, or leave the University.

Most of us who are caught in conflicts between what the organization wants and what we want are like Joe. Before we can begin to develop an effective course of action, we need to be aware of our feelings of distress, to recognize our defensive behavior, to confront our fears, and to examine our situation. The diagnostic questions you answered earlier will help you to examine your situation and will prepare you for an assessment of how your needs and values influence your behavior.

HOW TO ASSESS YOURSELF

Our approach to your personal assessment is designed to provide data which will assist you in determining your needs and values. Our daily behavior reveals what is important to us and provides insights into how we achieve what we want out of life. The following exercises present a structured process for increasing your self knowledge, by asking you to think about and describe your personal characteristics. After completing the exercises, you will have a more accurate picture of your needs and values. Then you will be in a better position to determine what is best for you.

DEVELOPMENTAL STAGE ASSESSMENT EXERCISE

Name ———————————————— Date ——————

Age ——————————————————————————

Instructions In the following questionnaire, there are eight sentence stems regarding various aspects of your life. Circle the letter which you feel most accurately describes your current behavior as *you* see it. Your response should be on the basis of how you think things *really* are, not on how you would like them to be.

In some cases, more than one statement may describe your current situation. However, you are to select the statement which is *most* characteristic of you.

DEVELOPMENTAL STAGE ASSESSMENT QUESTIONNAIRE

1 My main concern is:
   a becoming a contributing member of my chosen profession.
   b financial security for retirement purposes.
   c being able to fend for myself.
   d accepting what I have not achieved with my life.
   e taking advantage of my last chance to make it big.
   f selecting the right career.
   g finding out what I want out of life.

2 My interpersonal relationships are characterized by:
   a turmoil and change often being caused by my wanting to find out more about myself.
   b a desire for confirmation of my life choices.
   c a lack of excitement but a need for support; achieve recognition in my career.
   d stability and a sense of well-being.
   e being less intense and less substantive.
   f a need for support from my close friends.
   g a reawakening of the old dependent-independent feelings.

3 One of my dominant goals is:
   a maintaining my health.
   b achieving independence from my parents.
   c identifying what my life means to me and what I can do with the limited time I have left.
   d deciding what to do with my life.
   e making enough money to do what I want.
   f discovering what is right for me.
   g being active socially.

4 My primary value is:
   a security.
   b autonomy.
   c accomplishment/prestige.
   d independence.
   e self-identity.

    f commitment.
    g wisdom.
5 My life is:
    a full of an urgency to succeed.
    b not so rushed; it is a time for sharing human experiences.
    c unknown.
    d stable. What has been done, has been done.
    e for me to define and control.
    f passing too quickly. I have one last chance to make it.
    g uncertain and full of crucial decisions.
6 The future is:
    a uncertain and becoming increasingly important.
    b not as important as my being free from the external world of the present.
    c pressing in on me and I am running out of opportunities.
    d not as important as the present.
    e not important.
    f a time I fantasize about.
    g limited and I feel a time squeeze.
7 My career behavior is characterized by:
    a a developing taste for power.
    b a concern for power, politics, and influence.
    c learning about the world of work.
    d being a decision-maker.
    e being able to formulate and implement strategies for improving organizational performance.
    f a concern for being remembered when I retire.
    g identifying my competency and understanding elements of leadership.
8 My identity is:
    a defined by how well I perform in my job.
    b torn between what I am now and wanting to change.
    c well-established with a feeling of relief.
    d questioned and related to the meaningfulness of my life.
    e closely related to my family.
    f well-defined even though I may not be completely satisfied with it.
    g something which I don't seem to have control of.

SCORING THE DEVELOPMENTAL STAGE ASSESSMENT EXERCISE

Directions: Circle the letters below which you circled for each item of the questionnaire.

Stages of Adult Development

Item	1 Pulling-up roots (16-22)	2 Provisional adulthood (22-29)	3 Age-30 transition (29-32)	4 Rooting (32-39)	5 Mid-life transition (39-43)	6 Restabilization and flowering (43-50)	7 Mellowing (50-60+)
1	c	f	g	a	e	d	b
2	f	b	a	c	g	d	e
3	b	d	f	e	c	g	a
4	d	f	e	c	b	a	g
5	c	e	g	a	f	d	b
6	f	d	a	g	c	b	e
7	c	g	a	e	d	b	f
8	e	f	g	a	b	c	d

Total number of items circled in each column _____

The column with the highest frequency of circled items indicates the stage of adult development most characteristic of your behavior. The tasks of each stage are described in Chapter 2.

WHAT THE DEVELOPMENTAL STAGE ASSESSMENT CAN TELL YOU

Determining your stage of development, and tasks characteristic of that stage, can tell you whether your behavior is typical of other adults of a comparable age. If your assessment places you in a category that is different from what other adults of a comparable age are experiencing—i.e., you are ahead of or behind others in your development—your discomfort may be the result of having to deal with inappropriate tasks. If your stage of development places you in the appropriate age grouping, your feelings of distress may be caused by a questioning of your life's goals and beliefs, which are characteristic of each developmental stage. Such information can help you cope with your life-tasks and can help show you what needs to be done to get you through that stage.

While each stage is general and reflects averages, differences do appear in our development. As we related earlier, the common denominator of the changes we experience is *what* we face not *how* we face it. What the developmental stage assessment helps you to determine is:

1 Life tasks appropriate to your stage of development.
2 What obstacles you need to overcome.
3 That your feelings of distress may be "normal," and that you just need to "hang-in-there."
4 How to point out specific actions you can take to help achieve your primary developmental task.
5 That your feelings of distress are not caused by your organization or some wrong decision you made.

IDENTIFYING OUR NEEDS AND VALUES

Assessing our stage of development and tasks is the first step in clarifying what factors contribute to our behavior. The next step is to identify our needs and values. The following set of exercises is designed to help you look at your needs and priorities from your own unique frame of reference. The first two activities, based upon J. O. Stevens' (1971), *Awareness*, help us begin identifying what our needs are.

In the space provided below, fill in as many "need" statements as you can. Then, fill in as many "want" statements as you can.

Things I need	Things I want

When you have finished, compare the lists. Is there any overlap? Substitute the word "want" for "need". What happens? Are some of your wants, needs? If our needs can be modified to wants, the pressure is reduced in terms of our having to create situations to satisfy those needs. We will have more options. We can own and control our "wants," but our "needs" own and control us.

In Joe's case, he wanted to remain at the University. He wanted to maintain his identity. He wanted to be respected by his colleagues; however, he could survive without them. He had another job offer. His livelihood was not dependent upon the University. Knowing this, Joe could begin to search for alternatives.

The same was true of Jean; she wanted to change her career, but she did not need to in order to survive. By controlling her wants, she was able to search for alternatives and risk the change.

The following exercise should also help you explore your wants further. List as many "things you have to do" in the appropriate column. Then, list as many "things you choose to do" as you can. Now, substitute the word "choose" for the word "have." Read over the list with the new heading. What reactions do you have?

Things I have to do	Things I choose to do

As you review the lists, what may begin to happen is the realization that what you perceive as "having to do" are actually behaviors that you "choose to do." What we choose to do, we can control. By being able to control our behavior, we can change. As we begin to take responsibility for our feelings and behavior, the number of options and alternatives we have, increase. The result is a liberating experience, which reinforces our involvement in the self-assessment process.

In order to clarify your choices, you need to clarify your values. We can hardly understand what our goals are without being aware of the choices we have already made. Our past decisions reflect our value structure. If we have been responding and making decisions based upon a set of values that have been hidden from us, we have been moving in directions that we do not understand or are dissatisfied with. Through the use of value clarification, we can begin to identify our priorities.

In Chapter 2, we showed that values can be classified into three categories—physical, emotional, and intellectual. Figure 5.1 presents a review chart of the three types of values and their characteristics.

As you progress through the value-clarification exercise, we will be asking you to classify your values into these three categories. When you begin the exercise, keep the above definitions in mind.

Values	Characteristics
Physical	Activities which have a physical effect on you—e.g., exercise, movement, working conditions on the job, recreation, and effort required.
Emotional	Ideas and attitudes we feel about ourselves and others—e.g., importance of family, personal relationships, helping people, and value of life.
Intellectual	Relates to our cognitive processes—e.g., creativity, reading, abstract thinking, and decision-making.

Fig. 5.1. Values and their characteristics.

In order to identify our priorities, we need to rank-order our values. Our behavior is changed and influenced in the way we establish our priorities and values. The goal of the following exercise is to help us become more aware of our value-ranking—i.e., our priorities.

In each column of values, select and circle five values you feel are representative of your value system. If you want to add additional values to the list which present a more accurate description of your value system, please add them in the space provided.

VALUE CHOICE LIST

Physical values	Emotional values	Intellectual values
activity	responsibility	learning
body use	stability	creativity
comfort	prestige	complexity
travel	competition	decision-making
appearance	commitment	computation
money/reward	equality	abstraction
vacation	security	accomplishment
prosperity	trust	wisdom
strength	intimacy	independence
health	caring	rational
attractiveness	love	perfection
privacy	friendliness	planning
living conditions	compassion	reading
working conditions	openness	communication
body conditioning	involvement	completion
_____	_____	_____
_____	_____	_____

The next step is to rank-order your values and assign a weighting factor to each value. Write your values, in order, in the space provided below. Next, weight each value on a 0–5 basis, to reflect how important that value is to you.

Physical Values   Weight

1. _____   _____

2. _____   _____

3. _____   _____

4. _____   _____

5. _____   _____

Emotional Values   Weight

1. _____   _____

2. _____   _____

3. _____   _____

4. _____   _____

5. _____   _____

Intellectual Values   Weight

1. _____   _____

2. _____   _____

3. _____   _____

4. _____   _____

5. _____   _____

After you have completed the above exercise, you will have a clear picture of what your priorities are. In the next exercise, we are going to help you determine whether your past decisions and values have been congruent, i.e., have your decisions helped or hindered your feelings of well-being.

In the space provided below, list five decisions you have made in your life which you feel have had an impact on the type of life you are leading today.

Five Life Decisions

1. _____
2. _____
3. _____
4. _____
5. _____

From the rank-order list of your values, select the five values you feel are the most important to you. They may be selected from all three of the categories or from less than three. Write your top five values in the space below.

My Most Important Values

1. _____
2. _____
3. _____
4. _____
5. _____

In the following chart, combine your five top values with your life decisions. In each cell, evaluate your choice as to whether it helped, hindered, or had no effect on satisfying that particular value. Evaluate the decision by using a + sign if it helped; a − sign if it hindered; or a ? if it had no effect on satisfying that value.

	Life Decisions				
Values	1	2	3	4	5
1.					
2.					
3.					
4.					
5.					

Now tally the number of +, −, and ? assessments you made and determine whether your decisions have been congruent with your values. There are 25 cells. Using 25 as the denominator, the numerator becomes the frequency of the selected evaluation symbol. The result is a ratio of what proportion of your values were realized in your choices. The higher the ratio, the more congruent your choices and values and the greater the probability of your choices being what is best for you. The lower the ratio, the less congruent your choices and values and the greater the probability of your choices creating stress, discomfort, and unhappiness.

As you review the chart, what reactions do you have? Have your decisions been congruent with your values? Do you see any source of conflict? How do you feel about the decisions you have made?

What may begin to happen after this brief exercise is that you begin to be aware of your belief structure and what is important to you. Also, you may begin to further explore how you have made decisions in the past.

WHAT THE VALUE CLARIFICATION PROCESS CAN TELL YOU

Our values are important because they ultimately determine our choices and influence our behavior. While our value system is an important contributor to our behavior, that system may not be clear to us; thus our decisions and behavior are characterized by floundering and a sense of powerlessness. As a result, we have relinquished control over our decisions. The value clarification process you just completed will help you to determine:

1. How your past decisions were influenced by your values.
2. What your priorities are.
3. What you need to achieve feelings of greater self-affirmation.
4. What you need from your organizational/personal life to be happy.

ASSESSING YOUR PERSONALITY STYLE *

In Chapter 2 we stated that an individual's behavior is organized around a central theme or goal which serves as a unifying force for his behavior. By examining the repetitive behaviors we engage in to achieve that goal, we can identify our personality style.

To help you assess your personality style, we would like to have you rate yourself on the following scales. Read each of the descriptions carefully. On the continuum below place an X at the point where you think you are at the present time. Work rapidly as your first reaction will probably be the most accurate.

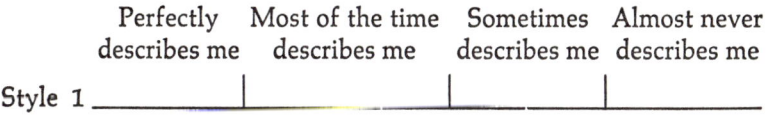

Style 1

—Seldom satisfied with one's achievements.
—Always has something to do; often has more than one project going.
—Difficult to relax; takes work home and on vacation.
—Always prepared to meet a new challenge.
—Accomplishes more than colleagues and brings it to their attention.

---

* Sperry, L., *Developing Skills in Contact Counseling*. Reading, Mass.: Addison-Wesley, 1975.

	Perfectly describes me	Most of the time describes me	Sometimes describes me	Almost never describes me
Style 2				

—Most projects do not turn out well.
—Important to have others one can depend on.
—Can be a procrastinator when faced with a task.
—Projects generally do not get completed.
—Needs constant supervision.
—Completed projects do not reflect competence of the individual.

	Perfectly describes me	Most of the time describes me	Sometimes describes me	Almost never describes me
Style 3				

—Really tries hard but often has ideas rejected.
—Sensitive and vulnerable to criticism.
—Looks for situations where there is a lack of respect for people and brings it to the attention of others.
—Often chooses friends who are strong and protective.

	Perfectly describes me	Most of the time describes me	Sometimes describes me	Almost never describes me
Style 4				

—Likes to be "Monday-morning quarterback" and plays it well.
—Generally does not lose arguments because he is well informed.
—Often says, "I told you so!"
—Seldom makes mistakes.
—Holds people to their end of the bargain and becomes indignant when they fail.

	Perfectly describes me	Most of the time describes me	Sometimes describes me	Almost never describes me
Style 5				

—Usually a well-rounded, well-liked person; knows how to get around.

—Has an insatiable urge to experience all there is in life.
—Feels entitled to the best service, care, products, etc.
—An ambitious person destined for bigger and better things.
—Knows the ins and outs of social grace; can be the life of the party.
—Knows how to get people to do things; can be clever, cute, and cunning.

	Perfectly describes me	Most of the time describes me	Sometimes describes me	Almost never describes me
Style 6				

—Takes pride in being very knowledgeable.
—Doesn't like mistakes made by anyone.
—Lets people know who the boss is.
—Doesn't usually show emotion; very level-headed.
—Often needs to step in to make sure the job is done properly.

The next step is to develop your *Personality Style Profile*. In Fig. 5.2, we have presented the personality style continuum. In the same area as you placed the X in the above exercise, place your six marks along the continuum for each of the six styles.

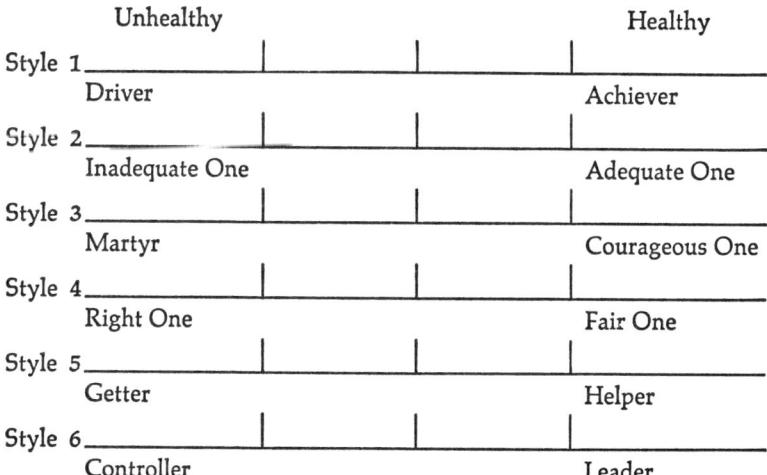

Fig. 5.2. My personality style profile.

For a description of each of the six styles, see Chapter 2. Your *Personality Style Profile* is designed to provide you with data concerning how you attempt to satisfy your needs and values. Specifically, this exercise will help you identify the following:

1 Why you act the way you do.
2 How you attempt to achieve your goals.
3 The composite parts of your personality.

YOUR PERSONAL VALUE INDEX

You have completed self-assessments in three areas. Each area contains a value component. What you need to look for are the common values which tie the pieces together. What you'll identify is a common set of values which you'll use when making your decision in Chapter 8. This set of values is called your Personal Value Index and represents your perceptions of where you are now.

Look back over your work. What are your common values? What do they tell you about yourself?

THE CASE OF RON AND JANET SAMUELS

The case of Ron and Janet Samuels is an example of how to fit the self-assessment results into the Personal Development Strategy (PDS). The first step in developing a PDS is a review of the current situation.

Ron and Janet were married when they were both 19. During their 11 years of marriage, Ron received his degree, enrolled in an evening MBA program, and was promoted from district to regional manager. Janet, due to an early pregnancy, dropped out of college, raised their children, and performed the normal tasks of a housewife. Ron felt that, during the past two years, they had been growing apart and had less and less in common. Ron "thought" he still loved his wife, but he found himself being quietly embarrassed when they socialized with his business associates, whose wives were college graduates and active in the arts and community. Ron felt guilty about having closed off Janet's chances to finish college, but he knew that things could not continue as they were. Ron's problem was to find out what he could do to resolve his marital problem. The first step was to assess his behavior and needs and values.

His first step in the self-assessment process is to discover what tasks he needs to confront as a 30-year-old person. By completing the Developmental Stage Assessment Questionnaire, Ron discovered that his descriptions of his current situation placed him in Stage 3, Age-30 Transition. Six of his responses were in Stage 3; two were in Stage 4, Rooting. The primary tasks of Stage 3, as presented in Fig. 2.2, are searching for a personal identity, reassessing future objectives, and searching for a meaning in life. Commitments are reassessed and the work of making choices involves great change and unrest. From this assessment, Ron discovered that his feelings were pretty similar to those of many other people at his stage of development, and that they were *normal*. This gave Ron the courage and hope to continue his search for an answer to his marital problem. It also suggested that Ron needed to master this task if he were going to successfully master later tasks.

To assess his needs and values, Ron completed the values clarification exercise. The results are a weighted ranking of his important physical, emotional, and intellectual values. Ron rank-ordered and weighted the following values:

Values	Weights
Physical:	
1. comfort	5
2. attractiveness/ physical appearance	4
3. health	4
Emotional:	
1. security/family	5
2. prestige	4
3. intimacy	3
Intellectual:	
1. wisdom	5
2. reading	3
3. perfection	3

Finally, Ron needed to complete his *Personality Style Profile*. His completed profile follows:

Psychologically Unhealthy					Psychologically Healthy
(Lo Synergy)					(Hi Synergy)
Driver				X	Achiever
Inadequate One			X		Adequate One
Martyr			X		Courageous One
Right One	X				Fair One
Getter		X			Helper
Controller	X				Leader

Reviewing his self-assessment, Ron began to develop a more complete picture of what he needed to be happy. He discovered that he was experiencing conflicts often characteristic of his stage of adult development, and that he valued comfort, security for his family, and wisdom. He was somewhat surprised that his personality style reflected a Right One-Controller behavior pattern. Ron had always considered himself to be an open, flexible person. It seemed that he needed to do something about that part of himself.

Before he can take any action, Ron needs to assess his marriage to determine whether his needs and values match Janet's. The following chapter will describe the process which Ron can use to assess his marriage. It may be helpful for Ron to view his marriage with the characteristics of an organization in order to assess it more objectively.

Chapter 6

Understanding Your Organization

The first step in developing your Personal Development Strategy is to "assess the situation" and your "reaction to it." You became a member of your organization because you thought it was good for you. If you were aware of better alternatives, you would probably be somewhere else. Now that you have gained an understanding of how your needs change and develop (Chapter 2) and have determined your current stage of need development (Chapter 5), you are ready to assess the organizational environment you are enmeshed in to determine whether it is capable of providing you with the nourishment you now need.

It should be evident after reading the previous two chapters that there is little reason to assume that just because the organization you joined two, five, or ten years ago satisfied your needs then, that it still does today. Organizations change and develop (Chapter 3) just as individuals do. This implies that the same match which existed in the past is unlikely to exist today. Now that you have a handle on your present need structure, it is necessary to assess the organization's stage of development and climate to see if a new match exists or can be realistically brought about by palatable adjustments in yourself or your organization.

In order to determine whether you are in a nurturing environment or not, you must assess your organization's ideologies, reward systems, procedures, and opportunities. This means objectively discovering how the organization actually operates, what it wants from you, and what it does to get it, which may be quite different than it wants you to believe, or than you want to believe.

Organizations have ways of socializing us to implant in our heads certain beliefs, attitudes, and ways of behaving which they think are in their best interests. These methods are easy to accept and hard to get rid of because they are reinforced by the organization through formal mechanisms, such as pay increases, promotions, demotions, and job assignments, and through informal means like approval and disapproval.

It is also hard for us to accept the existence of discrepancies in what we perceive, as well as the organization's "line" about what exists, because once we have incorporated these beliefs, attitudes, and ways of behaving into ourselves, we begin to believe that they are reality and are best. It is difficult for most of us to accept what the perceived discrepancies tell us. They may be saying that we have operated on false assumptions over the years, or that we have been wasting our time in dead-end situations. Or, they may indicate that things have changed and that we now must make difficult changes ourselves—that is, we must accept the fact that we cannot achieve what we had hoped for, or that we must sever ourselves from this organization, etc. As indicated earlier, it is often easier to "do nothing" than "do something" when confronted with unpalatable circumstances. But playing "ostrich" is never a fruitful long-run strategy; it does nothing more than provide a temporary reprieve before confronting the situation.

Whether the new awareness you receive from assessing your organization provides you with insights that confirm your worst expectations or revelations of undreamed-of opportunities, it is a necessary step in your Personal Development Strategy. Walking blindly through a shifting terrain can only by some very lucky circumstances take you on the best path for you. Determining "where your organization is really at" can be a consciousness raising experience that allows you to break out of its socialized assumptions. This awareness will allow you to see traps and opportunities, and will provide the knowledge necessary to determine what features of your organization are in your best self-interest, if any.

HOW TO ASSESS YOUR ORGANIZATION

The approach proposed for organizational assessment is designed to provide data which will assist you in determining strengths and weaknesses in your organization from your frame of reference. Your daily experiences would reveal the hidden perspectives you need to assess your organization, if you only know how to interpret them and took the time to do it.

The following Organization Assessment Exercise presents a structured means for increasing your insights by methodically asking you to think about and decide on the important characteristics which exist in your organization. After completing this exercise you will have a more accurate picture of your organization's values, expectations, and opportunities. Then you are in a position to decide whether it provides a congruent environment for your own needs and values.

ORGANIZATIONAL ASSESSMENT EXERCISE

Name ——————————————— Date ——————

Organization ———————————————————

Instructions: The following 10 sentences apply to various aspects of your organization. Circle A, B, C, or D to indicate the phrase which best completes the sentence that describes your organization as you see it. Your selection should be made on the basis of how you think things *really* are, rather than how you would like them to be or how the organization wants you to think they are.

Even though in some cases more than one phrase may describe your organization, please select only the predominant response.

ORGANIZATIONAL ASSESSMENT QUESTIONNAIRE

1 The main management concerns are:
   a creating products and markets.
   b instituting direction and efficiency.
   c delegating responsibility and coordination.
   d innovation, problem-solving, and interpersonal collaboration.

2 Communication is mostly:
  a formal and impersonal.
  b infrequent and written.
  c spontaneous and personal.
  d frequent and informal.
3 Control is usually based on:
  a plans, resource allocations, and formal systems.
  b social expectations and mutual goal setting.
  c immediate marketplace feedback.
  d accounting systems, budgets, and work standards.
4 Motivation is most often based on:
  a feelings of team accomplishment and team bonuses.
  b hope of partial ownership.
  c individual bonuses.
  d stock options, profit sharing.
5 Organization is mostly:
  a informal.
  b centralized and functional.
  c decentralized and line-staff.
  d cross-functional, problem-oriented.
6 The most predominant value is:
  a dominating and controlling opposition.
  b being rational and orderly.
  c serving the needs of members.
  d achieving a superordinate goal.
7 People act mostly to:
  a meet expectations of correct behavior.
  b do their own thing.
  c solve problems and accomplish tasks.
  d secure their personal advantage.
8 Relationships with other organizations are based mainly on:
  a mutual interests and congeniality.
  b collaboration.
  c competition.
  d agreements and laws.
9 Authority is mostly derived from:
  a expertise.

    b ability to reward and punish.
    c position.
    d ability and willingness to help others.
10 People are rewarded most for:
    a ability to fight and win.
    b adhering to rules and procedures.
    c helping others.
    d contribution to organizational goals.

SCORING THE ORGANIZATIONAL ASSESSMENT EXERCISE

Directions Circle the letters below which you circled for each item of the questionnaire.

ORGANIZATIONAL STAGE OF DEVELOPMENT AND CLIMATE ORIENTATION

Item No.	Creativity (Task orientation)	Direction (Power orientation)	Delegation/ Coordination (Role orientation)	Collaboration (Person orientation)
1	a	b	c	d
2	d	a	b	c
3	c	d	a	b
4	b	c	d	a
5	a	b	c	d
6	d	a	b	c
7	c	d	a	b
8	b	c	d	a
9	a	b	c	d
10	d	a	b	c

Total number items circled each column ___   ___   ___   ___

    The column with the highest frequency of circled items indicates the type of organization you have noted. Its characteristics are described in Chapter 3.

WHAT THE ORGANIZATIONAL ASSESSMENT CAN TELL YOU

Determining your organization's stage of development and predominant ideology is important because they affect its ability to meet your needs. If the organization's ideologies are different from your values, and if its predominant concerns and expectations are different from your own, neither will contribute as much as desired and both will be dissatisfied. Specifically, the organizational assessment provides you with the data necessary to determine the following:

1. Predominant organizational values
2. Organizational goals
3. Expectations regarding appropriate ways of behaving
4. What kinds of control will be imposed
5. Qualities of organizational members which are valued
6. Appropriate ways of expressing yourself.

Figure 6.1 provides a framework for demonstrating the potential each type of organization has for matching values. Everyone, of course, has a unique set of values, which means that different people will be more or less satisfied in different types of organizations. But in general, Fig. 6.1 shows us that the Creativity-Task and Collaboration-Personal organizations offer the most potential for satisfying personal values—physical, emotional, and intellectual —for most people. Those of us who enjoy power and competition may be more happy in the Direction-Power type of organization. Others who prefer definite routines and low energy inputs might like to be members of the Delegation/Coordination-Role organizations. Those of us preferring opportunities for self-actualization and more intimate kinds of relationships, however, will usually find that the Creativity-Task and Collaboration-Person organizations best match our needs and values.

In *Creativity-Task organizations*, high physical activity is required to meet the demands for achievement, expectations of long hours of work, and needs for frequent interpersonal interaction. Emotional commitment to the organizational goals and its members is high and it is implemented by frequent and informal communica-

Type of organization	Personal values			
	Physical	Emotional	Intellectual	
Creativity-Task *High:*	long hours of work frequent interaction demand achievements	informal communication mutual goals strong emotional commitments	value creativity lots of intellectual application rapid information processing	
Direction-Power *Low:*	interpersonal competition causes high tension and anxiety energy committed to survival	impersonal hierarchy high insecurity no internal commitment	few key decision-makers creativity applied to discrediting others	
Delegation/Coordination-Role *Low:*	rigidly defined, limited physical activities energy output is just enough to get by	impersonal communication people valued only as role fillers no opportunities for emotional expression	rigidly defined narrow intellectual structures no creativity; rules define procedures	
Collaboration-Person *High:*	encouraged to be as active as can work according to personal preferences	oriented to personal fulfillment stress meaningful work high group commitments	application of talents encouraged increased education encouraged new innovations encouraged	

Fig. 6.1. Chances of matching personal values in four types of organizational settings.

tion. Creativity is valued in the application of intellectual abilities to new product and marketing ideas, and rapid information processing is required. Consequently, organizational expectations will match individual values which support high degrees of physical, emotional, and intellectual activity.

The same is true in the *Collaboration-Person organization*, which has the additional advantage of greater flexibility being allowed concerning the degree of physical activity and areas of application for intellectual skills. Individuals are encouraged to be as active as possible, but to work according to their personal preferences. Emotional commitments are high in collaborate groups, which stress meaningful work and are oriented towards facilitating the members' self-fulfillment. Intellectual-skill application is valued in innovations, and opportunities for increased education are provided.

In *Direction-Power organizations* the existence of extreme interpersonal competition results in high tension and anxiety. This requires a high degree of energy, but the energy is channeled toward survival, not toward achievement or creativity. The emphasis is on a few key decision-makers at the top of the power hierarchy, which leaves little opportunity for the application of others' intellectual skills, except when discrediting the skills of others. The "dog-eat-dog" environment also breeds a high degree of insecurity and low organizational or interpersonal commitments. This type of organization provides plenty of action for individuals oriented toward power and competition, but few rewards for other types of people.

In *Delegation/Coordination-Role organizations* physical activities are rigidly limited and defined. People are not expected to demonstrate more energy or commitment than defined by their role assignment. Communication is impersonal and few opportunities exist for emotional expression. Rules and procedures exist which limit intellectual activities and require no creativity. Individuals who can be happy in this type of organization are usually those desiring high security and minimal output of physical, emotional, or intellectual energy.

Your organizational assessment tells you what expectations, values, and opportunities exist for personal need fulfillment. Since you have already assessed your personal stage of development, values, and needs in earlier chapters, you can now compare them to the characteristics existing in your organization. For some of you, a suitable match will exist. You are in a position to do nothing! For others, however, it will be evident that there is a mismatch. If the latter is the case, the degree of mismatch must be determined in light of the information provided by your individual and organizational assessments. You will then have the necessary information to decide what to do about it—that is, try to change yourself, try to change the organization, or quit.

THE CASE OF JOE BRENNON

The case of Joe Brennon can serve as an example of how to fit the organizational assessment results in a Personal Development Strategy (PDS). In reviewing the situation (the first step in developing a PDS), it should be recalled that Joe was suffering psychosomatic symptoms based on his being turned down for promotion at his university, mainly because he did not fit the expected image of how a business professor should dress and appear. Joe's problem was how to make a decision that would satisfy conflicting physical, emotional, and intellectual values. To facilitate this decision the PDS model suggests that further information be generated through self and organizational assessments.

The next step is for Joe to do an assessment and clarification of his values and needs. The results are a weighted ranking of important physical, emotional, and intellectual values.

Let's assume that Joe rank-ordered and weighed on a 1–5 scale (1 being low and 5 high) these values:

Ranking	Weights
Physical:	
1. "Open" dress and behavior code	5
2. Salary and merit	5
3. Time and facilities for physical conditioning	3

(cont.)

Ranking	Weights
Emotional:	
1. "Open" climate for discussion/dissent	5
2. Support and encouragement from colleagues	3
3. Family settled and secure	3
Intellectual:	
1. Intellectual challenge of colleagues	4
2. Encouragement and help in doing research	2
3. Adequacy of research and library facilities	1

To assess the university's stage of development and value system, Joe completed the Organizational Assessment Questionnaire described in this chapter. The results were eight B's and two C's, indicating that Joe's organization was predominantly Direction-Power oriented, with some Delegation/Coordination-Role characteristics. As can be seen in Fig. 6.1, the chances for matching the personal values of someone like Joe to those of this type of organization are extremely low. The results of these personal and organizational assessments indicate a mismatch, which confirms what Joe was experiencing. Now, however, he has concrete and in-depth information regarding both himself and his organization which he can use to make a decision and formulate his PDS.

The next step for Joe is to fit this information into the Person-Organization Fit Decision-Making Grid so that he can decide what to do. The "do nothing" alternative is clearly impossible, given Joe's physical manifestations. The decision to leave, change himself, or change the organization, and how to implement this decision must still be confronted. The following chapter will describe this process and where to go from here.

Chapter 7

Making a Decision

So far you have made quite a bit of progress. You have assessed your own needs and values. You have examined your organization by looking at its values, expectations, and its written and unwritten codes. By now you are aware of the source of your dissatisfaction, as well as the satisfactions and payoffs that you receive by being part of that organization.

One more task is necessary before you can make an intelligent and informed decision about your future. You must first pool the various information you have gathered into a meaningful pattern. This pattern—called a decision-making grid—will serve as the basis for your decision-making and it will allow you to systematically compare the information you have collected about yourself and your organization.

YOUR FOUR OPTIONS

The way in which the informed person usually makes a decision is to generate two or more alternatives and then compare the courses of action. Often the alternatives are compared on paper, listing the advantages and disadvantages for each course of action in two columns usually called "pros" and "cons." At first glance this may appear to be a rather sophisticated and systematic approach. Unfortunately, many who have used this procedure have found that this method is too glib, too simplistic, and too likely to lead to premature, uninformed, and less than satisfying decisions.

For one thing, this pro and con approach does not systematically deal with one's values and needs or, when an organization is involved, with its expectations, values, and policies. There are almost always more than two options, and the pro and con approach does not allow one to compare all of the options at the same time. Very soon we will present a decision-making grid which will allow you to consider not only personal and organizational values, but also to compare any number of alternatives or options at the same time. First, a few words about options.

From our experience in working with individuals and organizations, it seems as though each individual has at least four options available when dealing with a problem. They are (1) stay and accept or accommodate the situation; (2) leave or get out of the situation; (3) change yourself; or (4) change the organization.

The *first option*—stay and accept or accommodate the situation—is sometimes called the "grin-and-bear-it" approach. This alternative is frequently a conscious choice, but more often it is an acquiescent one. For any number of reasons the individual may choose to "switch" rather than "fight," switching in this case means that the individual decides to suppress needs, change perceptions, or bring forth coping techniques to deal with the dissatisfying element.

Coping is the middle path between retreating and advancing. We look at the freeze on hiring in a department that is severely understaffed and we say: "Another 9 or 12 months and we should be out of the woods. I guess I can cope with it that long." Dr. Karl Menninger describes a number of coping strategies that we use to deal with short-term stress and disappointment, which range from eating more, working harder, blaming others, psychosomatic illnesses, rationalizations, and watching more television, to talking it over with friends. We know from experience that such coping devices can make our dissatisfaction seem more palatable, but they are not really long-term solutions. An effective set of coping skills, which we can call "survival skills," are needed for the longer term Survival skills are described in Chapter 9.

The *second option*—withdraw from the dissatisfying situation—may mean shifting departments or leaving the organization entirely. In either case, the decision to leave is based on the premise that the person can no longer continue to function, below some point-of-no-return, so that his or her needs can be met and values served. The process of leaving or quitting is a serious matter, and one that can involve psychological consequences such as separation anxiety or depression. Leaving often requires learning how to "let go." "Letting go" is briefly described in Chapter 9.

The *third option*—change one's self so that one's values become more harmonious with those of the organization—can also mean becoming more tolerant and accepting. Chapter 9 focuses on a variety of techniques and strategies that can be used to accomplish self-change and development of one's potentials.

The *fourth option* is to change the organization to better accommodate one's own needs and values. Planned change in an organization is referred to as organizational development. Chapter 10 focuses on a number of techniques and strategies that an insider can use individually or collectively to change the immediate organizational environment which the person finds dissatisfying.

These are the four most common options. There is another option for some sort of mutual change in the organization and the individual; however, dealing with such interactive changes is outside the scope of this book.

A DECISION-MAKING GRID

We previously mentioned the shortcomings of using the pro and con method of decision-making. We indicated that such an approach cannot systematically relate the needs and values of the individual and the organization or allow a simultaneous comparison of the alternative actions or options. In surveying a wide variety of decision-making models, ranging from the mathematical to the quasi-mathematical to the intuitive varieties, it became clear that none of these models were appropriate for the complex human problem-solving/decision-making that we are dealing with in this book. We therefore modified and restructured the problem-solving model presented by Robert Carkuff (1973) in a book entitled *The Art of Problem Solving*. We believe that Carkuff's model is by far the most comprehensive and sophisticated.

The value of this decision-making grid is that it helps one decide on a course of action based on a quantitative assessment of the person's needs and values. Let us suppose that you were a friend of Jean Lawrence and you were trying to help her decide among three courses of action: (1) remain at SOK Electronics as Vice President of Marketing; (2) enroll full-time in an interior-decorating training program; or (3) continue working at SOK and learn interior decorating on a part-time basis. Since we will first be presenting a slightly modified version of Carkhuff's model, we will only consider Jean's needs and values and not the values and dynamics of her business organization.

The *first step* in this decision-making process is to determine what is really important to Jean—that is, what her values are. This is accomplished using a value clarification and assessment procedure, where we help Jean list those values which she considers most important in the three categories: physical, emotional, and intellectual.

The *second step* is to help Jean rank-order her values in terms of their importance. For the sake of clarity and simplicity, let us suppose that Jean lists and rank-orders only two values under each of the three broad categories.

The *third step* is to assign a weight to each value in the three categories. This weighting is necessary because, even though Jean may cherish her first rank-ordered value twice as much as the second, she may give equal weight to a third or fourth rank-ordered value—if there were a third or fourth. A scale of 1 to 10 is suggested, where 10 is considered the highest value and 1 the lowest; but perhaps it might be more useful to assign weights based on another criterion, such as time. For example, we could help Jean assign weights based on the amount of time (in hours) that might be associated with a particular value in a given day or week.

Suppose that Jean's rank-order of the four values in the Physical category is as follows:

1 Salary.
2 Time for leisure and friends.
3 A spacious and impressive office.
4 A flexible schedule.

We learn from Jean that salary is about three times more important to her than the status of a large office. So she assigns a weight of 9 to her salary and 3 to the spacious and impressive office. She feels that flexibility in scheduling her hours is about as important as her office, so she assigns it a value of 3. But for Jean, having enough free time to spend with friends and leisure is almost as important as money, so she assigns it an 8. We would then proceed to help Jean assign weights to the other areas.

The *fourth step* is to specify alternative courses of actions. Initially, Jean thought she had three: (1) stay at SOK; (2) study interior decorating; or (3) stay at SOK and study interior decorating part-time. If there are other alternatives, they should also be listed. These alternatives will form the horizontal dimension of the grid, while the values will form the perpendicular dimension.

The *fifth and last step* is to determine whether each alternative course of action or option, helps or hinders each particular value. This is accomplished by assigning the signs −, +, 0, −−, or ++ to each point of interaction on the grid. The meaning of the signs is as follows:

− − severely hinders the value
 − slightly hinders the value
 0 does not hinder or help the value
 + slightly helps the value
++ greatly helps the value

Let's say that Jean assigns the following values, weights, and signs to each of the three alternatives: (See Fig. 7.1.)

As you can see in Fig. 7.1, the signs have been multiplied by the weights. The products were then added to yield the cell totals. The final step of the decision-making process is to decide on one of

116 Making a Decision

Values		Courses of action—options		
Ranked values	Weights	Stay at SOK	Training program (full-time)	SOK and training program (part-time)
Physical:				
1. Salary	9	+ (9)	−− (−18)	− (−9)
2. Leisure time	8	++ (16)	++ (16)	−− (−16)
Emotional:				
1. Autonomy	10	0 (0)	++ (20)	+ (10)
2. Communication among peers	4	+ (4)	+ (4)	− (−4)
Intellectual:				
1. New learning	9	0 (0)	++ (18)	++ (18)
2. Challenge	6	0 (0)	+ (6)	++ (12)
Cell totals		+19	+60	+11

Fig. 7.1. Jean's decision-making grid.

the three options or courses of action. Ideally, the best decision is to choose the option having a cell total that is approximately 65 percent of the Ideal Score. The Ideal Score can be derived by multiplying each value weight times the highest possible sign (++ or 2). In Jean's case, the Ideal Score is 92 (9×2 + 8×2 + 10×2 + 4×2 + 9×2 + 6×2 = 92). So for Jean, deciding to enter the interior-decorating training program and resign her present job appears to be the course of action that will best meet her needs and values. Had Jean's highest cell total been less than 65 percent of the Ideal Score—that is, less than 59—it would indicate that the option was not significantly different from the other options for Jean to accept it without qualification. And, when an option doesn't *significantly* outweigh the other alternatives, there is a good likelihood that a person like Jean hasn't very clearly examined and clarified what is really important to her—her values—or she has not accurately assessed the degree to which these valued behaviors are important to her. Our experience shows that a decided course of action must be significantly different from the other choices, in order for doubt to be reduced and real satisfaction to be possible. In such an instance, Jean would have been cautioned to *refine* both her value rank-order and weights, or to *review* the courses of action. The quantitative process would then be repeated and hopefully a clearly superior course of action would result.

THE MATCH-MISMATCH INDEX

As we previously pointed out, job satisfaction seems to be intimately related to the congruity or match between the person's values and his perception of the organization's values and structure. On the other hand, our thesis is that dissatisfaction seems to be closely related to the lack of congruity or mismatch between the person's values and his perceptions of the organization.

Research literature describes many pilot programs and experimental studies that have been conducted with the express purpose of trying to make work more meaningful and satisfying. The hope has been that if job satisfaction can be increased, absenteeism, alcoholism, pilferage, accidents, and the like, will be decreased, and worker morale and productivity should increase. Various ingenious innovations have been tried, among them are job enrichment and job redesign, training managers to change their style of management, flexible scheduling, shortening of the work week, and even going back to increased fringe benefits and pay. But none of these innovations have proven to be the sought-after panacea. There has been evidence that increasing the job satisfaction of employees can increase the effectiveness of organizations. Satisfied employees are absent less, late less, and less likely to quit. However, the research does not show that these employees work harder or produce more than do dissatisfied employees. In fact, there is some research which shows that once the novelty or halo effect of an innovation wears off, things pretty much return to the way they were.

Follow-up research on such studies usually shows that if the program did not adapt to the needs of the individual employees involved, little if any lasting change was evident. On the other hand, when innovations were adapted to the unique needs of each employee, and the employees, by and large, sensed that their job could be a place where people could grow and develop, organizational effectiveness was improved along with employee satisfaction and morale.

Thus it is the express purpose of this book to help you to better understand your own unique needs and then do something about them within the context of your organization. We hope to give you the necessary tools which will enable you to be your own change agent and to initiate change rather than wait for it to happen. As you know by now, we feel that the Personal Development Strategy and the skills it entails can be your most potent avenue for getting what you want and need.

Decision-making is the crucial phase of the Personal Development Strategy. In the person/organization decision-making grid that we will very shortly present, the Match-mismatch Index is at the heart of this system. The Match-mismatch Index is important for a number of reasons. First, it allows you to view the interaction between you and your organization in terms of a qualified index. This index suggests the degree of commonality or similarity between the individual's own perceptions and his perceptions of how the organization views the individual's values and needs. A high Match-mismatch Index suggests that there is much similarity of perception, while a low Index suggests that the organization will not or cannot encourage the individual to satisfy this value. The Match-mismatch Index is derived from the rank-orders of the assessments of one's personal values and needs and those of one's organization, and multiplying by the numerical ranking for each specified value. Let's take the case of Joe Brennon as an example. After doing an assessment and clarification of his values and needs in each of the three categories—physical, emotional, and intellectual, Joe rank-ordered and weighed on a 1–5 scale (1 being low and 5 high) the following values:

Ranked values	Weights
Physical:	
1. "Open" dress and behavior code	5
2. Salary and merit	5
3. Time and facilities for physical conditioning	3
Emotional:	
1. "Open" climate for discussion/dissent	5
2. Support and encouragement from colleagues	3
3. Family settled and secure	3
Intellectual:	
1. Intellectual challenge of colleagues	4
2. Encouragement and help in doing research	2
3. Adequacy of research and library facilities	1

In reality, Joe might have been able to generate and rank-order a list of five or even ten values in each of the three categories. For clarity's sake, we have confined our example to the nine values listed above.

We will assume that Joe completed an assessment of his organization as described in Chapter 6. From this assessment of the organization's stage of development and related value system, as well as Joe's knowledge of the organizations written and unwritten rules and policy, reward and support systems, and the payoffs that Joe receives from that organization, we ask Joe to assign weights to his rank-ordered values *as he perceives the organization would weight them,* given their understanding of how Joe and his needs and values "fit" into the organization's structure, ethic, and needs. Following is Joe's perception of how his department would have weighed his values:

Ranked values	(Organization) Weights
Physical:	
1. "Open" dress and behavior code	1
2. Salary and merit	2
3 Time and facilities for physical conditioning	4
Emotional:	
1. "Open" climate for discussion/dissent	1
2. Support and encouragement from colleagues	1
3. Family settled and secure	5
Intellectual:	
1. Intellectual challenge of colleagues	2
2. Encouragement and help in doing research	1
3. Adequacy of research and library facilities	4

You will note there are some rather wide discrepancies between the two sets of weightings. No wonder Joe feels dissatisfied, anxious, and out of place. The next step is for Joe to derive the Match-mismatch Index, multiplying the weights by each other:

	Weights (Joe)	× Weights (Organization)	= Match-mismatch index
Physical	5	1	5
	5	2	10
	3	4	12
Emotional	5	1	5
	3	1	3
	3	5	15
Intellectual	4	2	8
	2	1	2
	1	4	4

THE PERSON-ORGANIZATION DECISION-MAKING GRID

The final step is to transfer the value rankings and the Match-mismatch Index to the grid that we previously presented. You will note that the four options we discussed earlier in this chapter form the horizontal dimension. Figure 7.2 presents the decision-making grid for Joe Brennon's situation.

Now what does Joe's grid tell us? Actually, it provides quite a bit of information. First, it appears that Joe's best informed decision would be to resign his job. The score of 78 is nearly 65 percent of the ideal score of 128. It is interesting to note that the next highest weighted course of action is to change the organization. In other words, Joe's perceptions, taken collectively, suggest that the department's receptivity to change is much greater than Joe's own perception of his willingness to change, as far as these particular values are concerned. In fact, Joe's cell total of −65 on the "Change-Self" option suggests a dogged determinism to hang on to his values, at almost any cost. In terms of the personality-style types, Joe seems to be high on the Controller/Leader and Right-One/Just-One columns.

Finally, this grid suggests that the values on which Joe is "willing" to change himself on are the same ones he perceives the department willing to change on. This suggests that should Joe find that he must continue on with his job, there are possibly enough personal and departmental strengths that Joe can build on and working to change his organization in such areas as " 'open' climate for discussion and dissent" and "intellectual change of colleagues" seem to be possibilities for change.

Our advice to someone in Joe's situation who has decided to leave the organization would be to look very carefully at other job opportunities and evaluate them in terms of closeness to "fit." But, if Joe does not find it possible to leave, we would suggest that he look to the "Change Strategies" (outlined in Chapters 9 and 10) that relate to his particular situation. In terms of his Personal Development Strategy, Joe has completed the first four steps and should move on to the "Commitment and Achievement" steps.

In order for you to gain more experience in working with this Person-Organization Decision-making Grid, we will go through

Values			Courses of action—options			
Ranked values	Match-mismatch index	Ideal values	Stay	Leave	Change self	Change organization
Physical:						
1. Behavior code	5	10	—— (−5)	+ (5)	—— (−10)	— (−5)
2. Salary	10	20	—— (−20)	++ (20)	0 (0)	0 (0)
3. Conditioning	12	24	++ (24)	+ (12)	—— (−24)	++ (24)
Emotional:						
1. Climate	5	10	—— (−10)	+ (5)	—— (−10)	— (−5)
2. Colleague support	3	6	—— (−6)	+ (3)	0 (0)	++ (3)
3. Family	15	30	+ (15)	— (−15)	— (−15)	+ (15)
Intellectual:						
1. Challenge	8	16	—— (−16)	+ (8)	— (−2)	— (−8)
2. Research	2	4	— (−2)	+ (2)	0 (0)	0 (0)
3. Facilities	4	8	— (−4)	++ (8)	— (−4)	0 (0)
	Cell totals	128	−24	78	−65	24

Fig. 7.2. Decision-making grid for Joe Brennon's situation.

another example with you. The case of Dick Larson presents a much different picture than that of Joe Brennon. Dick's dissatisfaction is of a much different nature. You will recall that Dick felt upstaged by Fred Steggert, who, in many ways, has a Driver-type personality. For example, Drivers are hard working individuals who work most of the time, even at 2:30 in the morning! It is not unusual for a Driver-type personality to take on a project singlehandedly, while turning others off and engendering guilt feelings in them at the same time. James Halberson seems to have a strong Controller-type personality. And, when Controllers and Drivers team up, especially in highly demanding R & D work settings, dissatisfaction is likely to mount very rapidly. Now let's help Dick look at his situation, and his four options.

After completing an assessment and clarification of his values and needs in each of the three categories, Dick determines his value weights. We will also assume that he has completed an assessment of Lakeside, especially the R & D team, and has assigned Weights to his rank-ordered values as he perceived the organization would weight them. Below are Dick's data:

Ranked values	Dick Weights	Lakeside Weights	Match-mismatch index
Physical:			
1. Health and safety	4	3	12
2. Money	4	3	12
3. Comfort	3	2	6
Emotional:			
1. Security and caring	5	2	10
2. Equality	5	3	15
3. Assertive leadership	1	5	5
Intellectual:			
1. Open communication	5	2	10
2. Creativity	3	3	9
3. Accomplishment and achievement	3	5	15

Values			Courses of action—options			
Ranked values	Match-mismatch index	Ideal values	Stay	Leave	Change self	Change organization
Physical:						
1. Health and Safety	12	24	+ (12)	0 (0)	++ (12)	++ (12)
2. Money	12	24	++ (24)	+ (12)	++ (24)	++ (24)
3. Comfort	6	12	+ (6)	+ (6)	+ (6)	+ (6)
Emotional:						
1. Security and caring	10	20	−− (−20)	++ (20)	− (−10)	++ (20)
2. Equality	15	30	+ (15)	+ (15)	+ (15)	+ (15)
3. Assertive leadership	5	10	−− (−10)	0 (0)	0 (0)	++ (10)
Intellectual:						
1. Open communication	10	20	−− (−10)	+ (10)	− (−10)	++ (20)
2. Creativity	9	18	+ (9)	+ (9)	+ (9)	+ (9)
3. Achievement	15	30	+ (15)	+ (15)	+ (15)	+ (15)
	Cell totals 188		51	82	61	131

Figure 7.3

It becomes clear that there is little difficulty in the physical area. The most noticeable value difference or mismatch is in the emotional area, and somewhat in the intellectual area. The greatest mismatches seem to be in the area of assertive leadership, a sense of security and personal caring, and open communication.

We now transfer the value rankings and the Match-mismatch data to the decision-making grid. Figure 7.3 presents the grid for Dick Larson's situation, and his four options.

According to the grid totals, the fourth option, Changing the Organization, has the highest weight. The total of 131 is more than 65 percent of the ideal total weight of 188 so, according to the rule of thumb, this is Dick's preferred course of action. Dick's case will be further explored in Chapter 8. Change techniques and strategies appropriate to Dick's personality style as well as the structure and climate at Lakeside will also be illustrated.

Chapter 8

Implementing and Evaluating Your Development Program

Now that you have decided on a course of action, you are ready to move to the last step of the Personal Development Strategy. This last step involves putting your development program into operation and measuring its degree of change. You must plan as carefully for implementing the course of action as you did in the decision-making stage. The best way to implement a course of action is to develop a step-by-step program for achieving your goal. Having an adequate step-by-step program will not only increase the likelihood that you will achieve your goal, but it will also reinforce your *commitment* to this course of action.

Implementation is usually the most difficult stage in a change program for most people. At this point, the distinction between intentions and actions becomes most apparent. Many of us desire to change. We will even invest the time and energy in assessing our situation and engage in decision-making. But, then we stop! Logically, the next step should be easy—but it isn't.

We don't act because we are unsure of the consequences of our actions. In other words, we fear failure, or maybe even success. We are increasingly dissatisfied with our current situation; but, as bad as the situation is, we are still receiving payoffs. In the pit of our stomachs we experience a gnawing anxiety about the future. Can we make it? Is the risk and hard work really worth it? These feelings are very real and very natural.

If our development plan increases the probability of our succeeding and realizing the sought-after change, it is a good plan. Our systematic approach of implementing and evaluating—two processes we see as occurring simultaneously—is based on having realistic *performance criteria*. These performance criteria are the subgoal or steps in the change program. Now let us look at some criteria for personal and organizational development.

SELF-ACTUALIZATION AS A CRITERION

As we suggested in Chapter 4, self-actualization can be considered a very legitimate goal and criterion for self-development, if it is understood correctly. We pointed out that when self-actualization is defined as meaning "happiness seeking" or "doing one's own thing," satisfaction and a sense of fulfillment can never be achieved. It has been stated rather bluntly that: "The direct pursuit of happiness is a recipe for an unhappy life." But when self-actualization or, more accurately, self-actualizing, is seen as the fulfillment of self-transcendence, the by-product is individual and group satisfaction.

In Chapter 4 we also mentioned that when Maslow and his colleagues attempted to institute self-actualization as a goal for worker behavior, the results were equivocal. That is, some workers were unprepared, unwilling, or unable to behave in a self-directed and totally responsible manner, while others used the challenge to develop and actualize themselves. Perhaps the most important lessons to be learned from this discussion and research are the following:

1 Self-actualization means different things to different people.
2 Not all people or organizations can operate or want to operate at a self-actualizing level.

These two points reflect the basic thesis of this book which is that people only change when they experience a felt need to change, and that they usually change only in a direction that is consistent with their perceived values and needs and the payoff systems of the organization.

"ONE MAN'S MEAT IS ANOTHER MAN'S POISON"

Very few change agents seem to understand or accept this old truism. When an organization and its change agents succumb to the myth of the "average" person and standardize their innovative approaches to jobs and jobholders, trouble and disappointment are inevitably the outcome. When we are talking about criteria for measuring self-actualization and organizational development, we need to base all our goal setting and evaluation on the assumption that each person is "unique" and that his or her behavior is influenced by his or her environment.

It is on this basic assumption that we have based our discussion about "goodness of fit" and the "Match-mismatch Index." As you know, we feel that job satisfaction, personal competence, and organizational effectiveness is a likely outcome of "good fit." By "satisfaction" we don't mean some sort of mutual "I'll scratch your back if you scratch mine" mediocrity, but rather satisfaction that results from creative achievement and adaptation.

PERFORMANCE CRITERIA AND "BEST FIT"

It should be clear from the preceding discussion that, in and of itself, "self-actualization" does not seem to be a very helpful criterion for change. The reason for this is that unless the characteristics of self-actualization are operationalized or stated in ways that are within the individual's perceivable grasp, and also capable of being accomplished within the individual's organizational structure, the probability of success is small. Stated another way, unless the performance criteria are related to the person's needs, values, and organizational context, they are not likely to be personalized, internalized, or seen as really meaningful to the individual. Without this sense of personal meaning, commitment will be difficult; and, without commitment, the probability of successful action is minimized. Furthermore, continued action and success is not likely unless the action is rewarded and encouraged. In other words, a new set of personal and organizational payoffs must be built into the development plan. It is only then that success is possible.

What we are suggesting is that, instead of using a unidimensional concept like self-actualization, you use your value profile and perception of the match between your values and the values of your organization as the criteria for your development program. As we suggested in our discussion of values and personality styles in Chapters 2 and 5, value dimensions can be fitted to the Healthy/High Synergy-Unhealthy/Low Synergy continuum of personality styles. We encouraged you to profile your values and needs on the Personality-styles Chart.

Your value profile can be very helpful to you in setting up your development plan. It can serve as a point of reference in setting up subgoals and establishing new payoff systems. Your profile should help you to state rather explicitly what your performance criteria are.

As we stated in an earlier chapter, self-development, self-actualization, or self-transcendence can be operationalized as any movement beyond the midpoints of each value—need continuum that you find yourself functioning at. It may be helpful to illustrate this point with the case of Dick Larson.

	Psychologically unhealthy (Lo Synergy)	Psychologically healthy (Hi Synergy)
Primary systems	Driver————X	O————Achiever
	Inadequate One——X	O————Adequate One
	Martyr————X	O————Courageous One
Secondary systems	Right One————X	O————Fair One
	Getter————————	X O————Helper
	Controller————————	X O————Leader

Fig. 8.1. Personality-style profile for Dick Larson.

Let us say that Larson developed the following profile to characterize his values and needs. Figure 8.1 shows this profile. His current value dynamics are charted with "X"s.

In Chapter 7 we learned of Dick's decision to reconsider his precipitous resignation and return to Lakeside Laboratories, contingent on the resolution of "certain conditions." We will show you how Dick specifically stipulated those "conditions," which form the core of his development plan. In order for Dick to feel more satisfied and to view his interaction with his organization in growth terms, he would like the organization to "allow" *and* "encourage" him to develop himself, especially in the primary systems. To operationalize this goal—in other words, to be more specific—Dick wants his profile to look like the one indicated by "O"s. Before continuing with Dick's case let us lay out the steps involved in "Implementing and Evaluating the Development Plan."

STEPS FOR IMPLEMENTATION-EVALUATION

It is significant that implementation and evaluation are hyphenated. By using the hyphen we are attempting to suggest that both processes occur simultaneously. We are not interested in the "one shot, before-and-after" evaluation that is familiar to most of us. It is not helpful to know whether you changed or failed to change or changed by this or that degree or percentage. In this book we are concerned with real people—people who are in the process of making major life decisions and changes. Our main concern is helping you to change successfully. We are also interested in helping you make and implement developmental changes that are success-based and that have a high probability of success.

Our purpose in writing this book and encouraging you as you read to work through the exercises is to help you develop a very systematic schema for change that will minimize the possibility of failure. For this reason, it is important that the planning and implementation of your change plan have evaluation and feedback loops at every point. Evaluation can be thought of as being analogous to the self-correcting guidance system of a missile or to the radar or automatic-pilot devices of a commercial airliner.

The steps for implementing-evaluating a development program are as follows:

1. State the specific goal(s) for change.
2. Operationalize the goal(s).
3. Set up subgoals.
4. Build in payoff systems.
5. Set-up check steps.

For years behavioral scientists have written about program planning. Usually, they agree that Steps 1, 2, and 3 are the basic building blocks of a change program. To these three steps, however, we have added two more. From our study of organizational behavior and from the behaviorist's study of individual behavior, we have found that it is essential to consider maintenance, reward, and support systems. From Robert Carkhuff (1974), *How to Help Yourself: The Art of Program Development*, we have borrowed the fifth step—the "check-steps" concept.

Step 1: State the Specific Goal(s) for Change

In the fourth step of the Personal Development Strategy you actually begin the goal-setting process. After examining the problem situation and undertaking the various assessments, you decided on one (or more) of the four options, which constitutes your primary goal(s) direction. Now, it is necessary to break down the goal(s) direction into specific goals. In specifying the goal(s), you must keep in mind the relationship between physical, emotional, and intellectual functioning, the Match-mismatch Index, payoff systems, and your Personality Style Profile. State the goal(s) in terms of your decided option and in terms of your relationship with the organization. You may want to designate the change in functioning level on the primary systems of your Personality Style Profile as we did in the case of Dick Larson.

Step 2: Operationalize the Goal(s)

Now that you have specified your goal(s), you must "define" or "operationalize" it (them). That is, you must break your goal down into its component operations and specify it in observable, measurable dimensions. First of all, you must specify the categories of value behavior to be changed. Then, you must rank those behaviors in terms of their complexity or in terms of their time sequence. Rules of thumb for defining something in measurable terms are as follows:

1 *Who* is to do what?
2 *What* is to be done?
3 *When* is it to be done?
4 *How* will you *know* when it is accomplished?

An example of an operationalized goal is, "I will be able to type 30 words a minute by the end of the month, as determined by a standard ten-minute-timing test, to be administered by Mrs. Samuel, with no more than five errors."

Step 3: Set Up Subgoals

It is now necessary for you to break down each specific goal into its component dimensions. The reason for doing this is twofold. First, the process of specifying subgoals or substeps will help you to develop a clearer picture of just what has to be done to achieve a goal. Second, the process of specifying a subgoal and then achieving it is a built-in motivation, since each small success encourages a subsequent success. For example, if your goal is to increase your typing rate to 30 words per minute (assuming you have one month to increase your present rate of 20 words a minute and 10 errors), you might specify the following steps:

Subgoal

1 Work on typing speed during weeks 1 and 2 for 15 minutes per day, at 30 wpm.
2 Work on typing accuracy during week 3, with speed no lower than 20 wpm.
3 Work on typing speed and accuracy to the specified rates during week 4.

Step 4: Build in Payoff Systems

By now it should be clear that we believe that personal and organizational payoff systems are an essential component of organizational behavior. In your assessments of yourself and your organization, you analyzed the payoff systems and their effects. Now, it is necessary that you find ways to build alternative reward and support systems into your environment so that you will be able to replace the old payoffs with new ones. This step may take some time and creative sleuthing to find physical, social, and/or symbolic reinforcements and encouragements that have sufficient motivating strength and that "fit" your values and needs. For example, assuming that there are no organizational demands involved and that you are really motivated by playing tennis, you might set your payoff for meeting each of your subgoals as an additional set of tennis each week.

Step 5: Set Up Check Steps

Check steps, as described by Carkhuff, will help you to check out or get feedback on your program. They provide you with all the details you need to ensure that your development plan gets implemented. Check steps help you think about the things you will need before, during, and after you perform the subgoals. The check steps help you answer the following three questions:

1 What do I need to perform this program correctly?
2 Am I doing this correctly?
3 How well did I do it?

In the typing example, you might answer the first question, "I need a typewriter, at least 15 minutes of time to practice each day, a quiet place, paper, and a skill-building, self-teaching typing book." To the second question you might answer: "I'm doing this correctly if I am able to increase my speed and/or accuracy by following the skill-increment plan in the typing book, upon which I based my subgoals." To the third question you might answer: "I was able to meet each minimum weekly goal, and I exceeded my final timed test by 4 wpm."

THE CASE OF
DICK LARSON RESOLVED

So far, Dick Larson has decided to reconsider his resignation and return to Lakeside, since he now feels there is a very high likelihood that changes can be made at Lakeside. In terms of stating specific goals for change, Dick came up with the following:

1 Concerning the organization: The project team will set up performance standards for each member.

2 Concerning the organization: Communications between Dick and his boss will be improved.

3 Concerning the organization and Dick: Dick will increase his assertiveness. This will most likely be met with positive results on the job. This positive action will effectively develop more of Dick's Adequate One and Courageous One.

4 Corollary to Goals 1 and 3: Dick should develop his Achiever, since the performance standards and assertiveness should increase Dick's ability to resist being "hooked" by Mr. Halverson's Controller, which reinforced Dick's Driver in the past.

Now let's take two of Dick's goals and operationalize them. Dick defined his first goal in this fashion:

Dick will advise Mr. Halverson that he is setting up a Performance Standards Review Process* following the American Management Association format. This process of setting standards for performance will be initiated with a brief training seminar, which Dick will arrange before February 1. Dick will personally confer with each member of the project team about his or her performance standards for the next six months. Dick will set up standards for himself in conjunction with Mr. Halverson.

---

*
Performance standards are statements of conditions that will exist when a job is satisfactorily performed.

With regard to the third goal, Dick operationalized it as follows:

> Dick will participate in a two-day Assertiveness-Training Workshop to be sponsored by a local university during the month of January. Dick will attend both days of the conference, participate fully in all the lectures and exercises, and practice the assertive behaviors he learns at the conference at home and on the job.

Now, let us turn to the third step, Setting Up Subgoals. For Dick's first goal, the following subgoals were delineated:

a Inform Mr. Halverson of this plan by December 15.

b Finalize all arrangements for the Performance Standards Workshop by January 15.

c Personally announce and explain the reasons for the Workshop to each team member by January 10.

d Ensure that the Workshop has highest priority and make sure that it comes off successfully on the appointed day.

e Expect each team member to have a rough draft of his or her Standards for the period March to August ready by February 25.

f Meet with each team member, to come to a meeting of the minds concerning their standards, by March 5.

g Have a set of Standards prepared for Dick and meet with Mr. Halverson to discuss them within five days of their completion, by February 20.

The next step in the implementation process is first to build new payoff systems into the organization, and second into Dick's own personality. After a considerable amount of reflection Dick came up with the following statement:

> In the past, I seemed to be getting a lot of mixed payoffs (both negative and positive) from Mr. Halverson for being a Driver and overachieving, as well as for my "silent-suffering," Martyr behavior. When I resigned mysteriously, I guess I collected

more negative payoffs for my stoic suffering. And, of course, my Inadequate One really picked up on Fred's Controller-Driver. I can see now how I basked in my misery, thinking that Mr. Halverson and Fred "had it in for me." Wow! Anyway, it seems that I'll do well to use the objectivity of the Performance Standards as a criterion for not achieving more than I specified. And being able to spend more time at home with the kids and our new hobby should be pretty rewarding. Now I won't have any excuse for walking around the house worrying and moping. Having Performance Standards should cut down on my Right One, so it won't have to work double duty too much, any more. I should also be able to enjoy my role as project leader better now; there is quite a bit of prestige and a lot to be proud of in my accomplishments at Lakeside. Halverson sure enjoys his Controller-leader payoffs.

The last stage of the implementation-evaluation plan is to set up step checks. Here are the check steps that Dick set up for subgoal 1(b):

"What do I need to perform this correctly?"

1 Contact Apt Associates and confirm a Workshop date.
2 Set and post the schedule with secretaries, Dr. Halverson, team members, etc.
3 Schedule the conference room and have secretary take care of arrangements for coffee breaks.
4 Budget expenses.
5 Have secretary attend to all Workshop supplies and correspondence.

The questions: "Am I doing this correctly?" and "How well did I do it?" can only be answered as each of the five check steps are being completed and, of course, after they have been completed, when you can see the whole picture in perspective.

This then is the way the Implementation-Evaluation Stage of the Personal Development Strategy works. In the following two chapters you will be presented with a number of specific techniques and approaches to help you achieve your new goals.

Chapter 9

Strategies for Self-change

Ron Samuels was surprised when he discovered that his Controller-Right One had helped him get a promotion on the job, but had hampered his marital relationship. Ron prided himself on having the right answers, being knowledgeable, and being able to demonstrate to others the proper way of doing things. Suggesting books for Janet to read, offering helpful hints on how she could improve, and giving general advice on how she could become a better wife did nothing to change their relationship. Ron was unhappy in his marriage, but he wasn't quite ready to admit that the problem was his. The self-assessment exercises served to highlight the issue he had been trying to avoid. The problem was *his; his* needs were not being met; and, if things were going to improve, *he* had to do something about his behavior.

You may be in a situation similar to Ron's. Your organization may be satisfying your basic needs and values, and yet you are unhappy. You know that the organization doesn't have the problem; it's *your* behavior that is causing you difficulties. It may be that although you accept new assignments, you grumble about being taken advantage of. Or perhaps you wish that just once you could stand up to your superior and tell him what you really think. Or maybe many of your colleagues are "turned off" by your abrasive, "know-it-all" attitude. There are numerous examples of situations in which we find ourselves unhappy with the way we present ourselves. What is needed is a self-modification program, designed to help you select the personal-change strategy that is best suited to your desired goals and values. There are numerous behavior change strategies available; the ones we have selected are representative. They are appropriate when you desire to change, eliminate, or learn a new way of acting.

Before discussing specific behavior change techniques, it is important to discuss the implications of your "not doing anything" and remaining in your current position. Also, if you decide not to withdraw or let go, what can you do to prevent the reoccurrence of an unhappy situation? If you decide to change yourself, you should realize the importance of a commitment to changing your behavior. A commitment involves making a choice, giving yourself time to make the change, and holding yourself accountable for the change. And, you should be familiar with ten general guidelines for successful implementation of your selected self-change strategy.

SURVIVING

If your preferred action choice (based on where you are now) is to not do anything to change yourself or the organization but to "grin and bear it," the main advice we have for you is to stick with that decision as that is what seems best for you. The big question is, "How do you maintain your integrity without being overwhelmed by guilt feelings?"

To help you survive in your organization, there are coping techniques available, which will allow you to maintain a sense of dignity and not become overwhelmed by either your feelings of guilt or the power of the organization. Richard Byrd (1974) in his *Guide to Personal Risk Taking* suggests the following:

1 If you feel doubtful about your opinions, assume that your doubts are wrong, and that, in fact, yours is the only correct view. The idea is not to lie but to work at *not* creating doubt; state your views with confidence.
2 Stop grumbling and talking to yourself. Make your views known during the interview or meeting. Don't let your bad feelings fester inside you. Talk more to others when you're

tempted to talk to yourself. By not letting your feelings build up, you'll feel better.

3 Don't be such a good listener. If you have worked at becoming a good listener, you may find yourself not participating in the give and take with your colleagues, but pigeon-holed as "Mr. or Ms. Nice Person." Let your eyes wander! Look at your watch! Trade experiences! These behaviors will help you change the perceptions other people have of you. There is little risk involved, as most people act like that anyway, and you will probably feel much better if you do.

4 Don't accept the responsibility for anyone else's feelings. If someone tries to tell you they don't like what you have been doing, tell them that's their problem. You will be able to fend off those disguised requests by others who want you to be like them by telling them it's not your problem. Most of the critical feedback we receive from others is a disguised request for us to change. By telling the other person it's his or her problem, you put the responsibility where it belongs.

The point we are trying to make is that you can choose to stay and cope with your situation and still maintain your identity. However, you will have to work at it and it may be tough going. Besides the four strategies outlined above, Chapter 10 presents some additional techniques. The strategies used for changing organizations can also be used to help you survive. We refer you to that section for additional ideas.

LETTING GO

In many ways, the decision to withdraw by resigning or shifting departments is the most difficult to make. It involves giving up a known situation for something that is unknown. The risk is higher when we move in new directions. Yet, withdrawing is probably the choice many people make when they face a difficult situation. Dick Larson was a good example of withdrawal based on a fear of the present which overcame the fear of an unknown work environment in his new position.

If you decided to resign, withdraw, leave, or generally get away from it all, the main thing you need to work on is your *attitude*. When you enter a new situation, don't bring along the same set of expectations you held in your previous position, as they can only contribute to a repetition of your previous feelings of distress.

The most important activity you can engage in is identifying what is important to you and what you need to be happy. The self-assessment you completed in Chapter 5 should have provided you with that data. As you enter into new relationships and/or jobs, use that information as a basis for assessing your "fit."

DECIDING TO CHANGE

If your preferred action choice was to change, the big question now is, "How can I change my behavior and become a more satisfied person?" Let's look at what it takes to change yourself.

Commitment

"You want to change! So what! What makes it different this time? Why should we believe you when you say you are going to change? This is probably the second, third, fourth, or fifth time you have stated that you want to change!" Your answer to these questions is probably, ". . . but I *really* mean it. This time I am *really* going to change." For us it is not enough for you to say, "I am really going to change." There is a significant difference between what you want or would like to do and what you will actually do. An old expression says it well: "The road to hell is paved with good intentions."

No matter how realistic your desire or goal is, it remains little more than wishful thinking until you develop a contract to achieve your goal. The contract is intended to translate your *wanting* to change into determining *how* you are going to do it. What we are suggesting is that one of the main reasons people fail to change is that they don't know how. Deciding how to change is where most of the real problems start in self-change programs.

Most of us hesitate to take the risk and change. Even though we change constantly, there seems to be an inherent fear of change and we struggle desperately to maintain our position. For any of the strategies to work, the basic question you need to answer is,

"How much do you want the change?" The type of conflict we have between our intentions and our desires is aptly portrayed by Fritz Perls, a Gestalt therapist, as the "Topdog-Underdog" conflict. Perls (1969), writing in *Gestalt Therapy Verbatim* (p. 18), described the conflict as follows:

The topdog usually is righteous and authoritarian; he knows best. He is sometimes right, but always righteous. The topdog is a bully and works with "you should" and "you should not." The topdog manipulates with demands and threats of catastrophe, such as, "If you don't, then you won't be loved, you won't get to heaven, you will die," and so on.

The underdog manipulates with being defensive, apologetic, wheedling, playing the cry-baby, and such. The underdog has no power. The underdog is Mickey Mouse. The topdog is Supermouse. And the underdog works like this: "Mañana." "I try my best." "Look, I try again and again, I can't help it if I fail." "I can't help it if I forget your birthday." "<u>I have such good intentions</u>."* So you see the underdog is cunning, and usually gets the better of the topdog because the underdog is not as primitive as the topdog.

Viewing commitment from the topdog-underdog perspective helps us to understand the differences between intentions and desires and why it is so difficult to change.

What we advocate in helping you overcome the resistance to change is a written contract. The contract obligates you as to *how* you are going to change, *when* you are going to change, and *what* you are going to change. The contract specifies rules and spells out procedures. It is mainly a list of statements or rules telling you what you should or should not do. You might want to make an oral agreement with yourself or someone else, which might work some of the time. But your putting your rules in writing serves as a powerful tool and seems to have more binding power than a verbal agreement.

---

*
Underscoring is the authors' emphasis.

The contract holds you accountable for carrying out your self-change program. If you fail to perform, you will know where you have failed and what you can do to get back on the track again. Even though you may slip, it is important that you "hang in there." The contract helps you by spelling out what can be done to keep you moving. Development of your Implementation-Evaluation Stage of your Personal Development Strategy serves as your contract.

Commitment is the essence of any successful change program. Commitment takes you from the thinking and planning stages to the doing stage!

TIPS FOR BEING SUCCESSFUL IN SELF-CHANGE

If you have been thinking about changing, you probably have some good ideas about what you are going to do. Putting your thoughts into action, however, is another matter. One of the common feelings people who are attempting to change have is fear—the fear of not being recognized; the fear of being a fool; the fear that it won't make a difference. To help you overcome some of your fear of changing and committing yourself to action, the following principles can serve as helpful reminders when the going gets rough:

1 *Be open to new ideas.* As you begin to change your behavior, you will begin to notice that people respond to you differently. Being open to new ideas means suspending judgments on the new insights. Don't stereotype or confine yourself to the views of those close to you. Let the new ideas and responses come in and work themselves out.

2 *Live in the present.* We have to live right now. We need to be aware of our thoughts, feelings, and physical reactions to what is happening around us now. Living in the present involves being aware of how the people around you are thinking, feeling, and reacting. Your awareness of yourself and others will keep you anchored in "what is" rather than "what if."

3 *Use fantasy to predict success.* If you have ever participated in athletics, you have probably used this strategy. Prior to the

handball, racquetball, or tennis game, you probably imagined how you would hit the ball, what strategy to use to defeat your partner, etc. In essence, you played the game and defeated your opponent mentally before you even played the match. The same process can be used when you begin your self-change program. You imagine what hurdles you will face, how you can overcome them, where the challenges will come from, and what you will be like when you complete your change.

4 *Expect success.* Richard Byrd (1974), in his book, *A Guide to Personal Risk Taking,* uses the term "Immaculate Perceiver" to describe a person who has the only correct view. He says that if you assume all your doubts are wrong and work at not creating doubts, success has a better chance of occurring. Also, expecting success helps you to take advantage of the self-fulfilling prophecy. What you expect to happen, generally happens!

5 *Maintain some anchor points.* When you are in the midst of making changes in your life, try to keep some points stable. If you are having career problems and marital problems simultaneously, don't decide that it is time to sell the summer home or take on a new project. You already have two major problems to handle. Solve those problems before taking on new ones. When you being your self-change program, keep your attention on that and do not try to make major decisions in other areas of your life.

6 *Change is a process.* Growth occurs over time and in gradual fashion. There are going to be rough spots ahead. These techniques are only tools to help you develop. They will not produce results by themselves. The techniques interact with your behavior and that of others, over time, to gradually bring about changes. Some of the changes may not be what you expected. Keeping this principle in mind will help you to deal with the unexpected and will remind you that change occurs over time and is a process dependent upon other people as well as on yourself.

7 *Solicit feedback and advice from others.* Finding out how you are doing from others is necessary to help you evaluate the success of your change. Advice, especially from disinterested parties, can provide a fresh perspective on how you are doing. This can be crucial when you seem to have failed to bring about the desired change. Advice as to how you can break out of the stalemate, and feedback on how you are doing can get you back on track again.

8 *Have alternatives.* Nothing is more frustrating than to support an idea and then have it rejected. Being left with no alternatives takes you out of the game. Developing alternatives to unsuccessful behavior can help you to keep changing. It prevents you from being stymied. Alternatives provide options to behavior which doesn't seem to be working for you.

9 *Do it! Only make it work!* One of the most incapacitating attitudes of change programs is the person's expectation that there is only one right way of doing something. The person gets so worried about whether he or she is using the technique properly, that spontaneity is lost and he or she often gets tongue-tied and ceases any kind of action. What we are suggesting is that you should forget about whether you are using the technique properly. Judge your actions by how successful they are in aiding you to achieve your goals, not by whether or not you are using the strategy properly.

10 *Don't blame other people for your not doing anything.* There are consequences to changing our behavior. For example, if you decide to tell your superior what you are really thinking, you may be fired. While losing your job may be the outcome of your assertive behavior, your not standing up to him only serves to underscore your fear. If the consequences of your behavior change worry you and you decide not to do anything, your only recourse is to stop complaining about wanting to be different and work at accepting things as they are. You are the one who can make it happen, not the people around you. When you relinquish your control over your life and give others the power to satisfy your needs, you live in danger of losing your autonomy and individualism.

SELECTING YOUR SELF-CHANGE STRATEGY

The frustrations we experience with our organizations are frequently resolved by venting our feelings on colleagues, friends, and/or spouses. This catharsis provides short-term relief, but very little assistance in solving the problem. In situations where the source of the difficulty is the way we behave or don't behave, we need to actively work at changing our behavior, not just to complain about it. In this portion of the chapter, we will focus on what change strategies are appropriate for changing certain types of behavior.

In Chapter 2 we described six personality styles that are common in organizations. Each style reflects how a person tries to achieve his goals. In Chapter 5, we identified your personality style and constructed a *Personality Style Profile*. We also identified your needs and values as well as your dominant developmental tasks. In Chapter 7 you were assisted in selecting a course of action. At that point you decided that your action choice was to change your behavior.

Figure 9.1 displays some of the action techniques which are available to you to achieve that goal. The chart will help you identify what your problem is, what you want, and how you can get it. When you select your goal, the available strategies become easily discernible. You may select the strategy that you feel has the greatest potential for helping you, or you may want to combine two or more strategies. For example, combining modeling, role-playing, and assertiveness training into one action strategy would be particularly effective. This process leads from observing the behavior of another, to practicing the desired behavior in a controlled setting, to the actual doing stage.

The goal of any change strategy you select is to attain a state of congruence, or agreement, between your values and needs and your behavior. We often say, "Wouldn't it be nice...", or, "My life would sure be happier if...", or, "Gee, I wish I could...." Feelings of futility and helplessness are conveyed to the listener. The change strategy you select should help you to achieve your goals and to have more control over your life. The main point we are making is that there are specific things you can do to take away the feelings of being unhappy, dissatisfied, and/or frustrated.

	Desired outcomes				
Strategies	Improve self-esteem	Independence and confidence	Risk new behavior	More respectful of others	Flexibility and caring	More open and expressive
Physical conditioning	X	X				X
Relaxation	X					X
Sensitivity training				X	X	X
Assertiveness training	X	X	X			X
Psychotherapy			X		X	
Modeling	X	X		X	X	X
Role-playing	X		X		X	X
Bibliotherapy	X	X				X
Rational-behavior training		X		X		
Thought-stopping		X	X	X		

Fig. 9.1. Guide to selecting your self-change strategy.

Now let us look at the ten action strategies you can choose and how you can use them.

PHYSICAL CONDITIONING

Most of us pride ourselves on being competent and contributing people; yet we may be sluggish, feel bloated, or overweight, or suffer from indigestion and heartburn, or be depressed. Usually accompanying these signs are increases in drinking and smoking and a decrease in sleep. The simplest, and, in many cases, the only really effective strategy for dealing with these problems is physical conditioning—i.e., exercise and diet.

Dr. Kenneth Cooper (1970), an Air Force physician, has popularized exercises called aerobics. These exercises—e.g., jogging, handball, and bicycling—require tremendous outputs of oxygen. In *The New Aerobics*, it is Cooper's belief that we can make better use of the oxygen we inhale when we are in condition. The ability to command the extra oxygen needed in stress situations can make the difference between being productive or incapacitated.

Cooper presents evidence that a properly conditioned person can resist heart attacks, ulcers, hypertension, and respiratory problems better than the poorly conditioned person. Physical activity has also been demonstrated to be effective in treating mild cases of depression.

Cooper has established a program whereby each physical activity—e.g., running, handball, tennis—is worth so many points. A person should earn 30 points per week; this, according to Cooper, represents good, adequate physical conditioning. Cooper also emphasizes the important relationship between diet and exercise.

To determine what your current level of physical conditioning is, refer to Cooper's book or try the following two exercises:

Exercise 1

Directions: Sit quietly for five minutes, then take your pulse. The easiest way to accomplish this is to lightly press your thumb against the left side of your throat (on the carotid artery). Check the beat against the sweep second hand of a watch for

60 seconds. About 70 heart beats per minute is average. Sixty or fewer is considered good. Long-distance runners in top condition have pulses of 40 or so!

Exercise 2

Directions: Dr. Cooper suggests that you obtain a more accurate reading by seeing how far you can run on a flat surface in 12 minutes. "If you have been exercising regularly (that is, at least three times a week for a minimum of six weeks) and have been given the necessary medical clearance for your age... you may take the 12-minute test to determine your current level of fitness." He then gives fitness categories for different age groups of both men and women. The following example applies to men under 30.

Fitness category	Distance covered in miles
1. Very poor	Less than 1
2. Poor	1 to $1\frac{1}{4}$
3. Fair	$1\frac{1}{4}$ to $1\frac{1}{2}$
4. Good	$1\frac{1}{2}$ to $1\frac{3}{4}$
5. Excellent	$1\frac{3}{4}$ or more

When you have completed these exercises, you will have a good estimate of what your physical condition is. If your physical activity is lower than you would like, Cooper's book is a good reference for getting started. Also, if you experienced much physical discomfort, we recommend that you consult your doctor and establish an appropriate diet/exercise program.

DESENSITIZATION/RELAXATION

Many times the problems we encounter in our lives are caused by high levels of anxiety. The anxiety may be about speaking to large groups, fear of failure, job loss, or countless other matters. Desensitization is a change strategy that you can use to help overcome unpleasant emotional reactions to situations that are often seen by others to be nonanxiety producing. Thus anxiety may be the major reason why you are overly aggressive or overly achieving, or suffer from headaches or stomach distress, or have difficulty performing your normal, everyday tasks.

Desensitization is the process of reducing your anxiety and gradually bringing about feelings of comfort in the presence of what formerly caused anxiety. A person is taught, through relaxation training, how to experience positive feelings when confronted with anxiety-producing situations.

The objective of relaxation training is to teach yourself to relax in the presence of those situations which were formerly anxiety producing. For example, prior to having to present a verbal report to your superior on the success of your project, a situation which has always caused you severe anxiety, you take a few moments to relax your stomach muscles. Anytime you feel yourself getting anxious, select a muscle relaxation technique. Using it will help to reduce your anxiety and enable you to concentrate on the task.

E. Jacobson (1938), in a book called *Progressive Relaxation*, established the general format for relaxation training. With this technique, a person is helped to relax by successively tensing and then relaxing gross muscle groups throughout the body. The following format is often used.

1 From the hand and forearm muscles (making a tight fist)
2 To the biceps muscles (pushing down on elbow)
3 From the top part of the face (pushing up or down on eyebrows)
4 To the middle part of the face (wrinkling-up nose and eyes)
5 To the lower part of the face (gritting teeth to make a tight smile)
6 Then the chest muscles (taking deep breaths and forcing shoulder blades together)
7 Next the stomach (placing hands on stomach, pushing stomach muscles out against the hands)
8 Finally, the legs (extending legs out to full tension in thighs and calves)

The emphasis during relaxation training is for you to tense the muscle groups as tightly as possible. The state of tension is generally held for about 5 seconds and then the muscle group is immediately relaxed.

During the process we are about to describe, you should be seated in a comfortable chair or you may lie on the floor. Be sure to wear loose fitting clothing. We suggest that you make an audiotape based on the script below. Then turn on the tape and follow the instructions:

Sit comfortably. Position yourself so that your hands and legs are in a comfortable position. Take your time and get comfortable. (5 second pause) Good. It will be helpful if you close your eyes. Having your eyes closed is a way to help you relax. (5 second pause) Now start relaxing your hands. Tense the muscles of your hands as tightly as possible and hold them while I count to five: 1...2...3...4...5...Now relax your hands and let them hang limp. Just consciously let go and relax them, both of them. (5 seconds pause) Next your forearms. Tense the muscles as tightly as possible. 1...2...3...4...5...Relax...How do your arms feel?...so light and warm ...Now concentrate on and across your shoulders. Push your shoulders up as far as they'll go. Hold it...

Okay, relax. Now think about the back of your neck. Tighten your neck muscles...Hold it...1...2...3...4... 5...O.K. Now relax your neck muscles. Feel that warm tingling sensation? Now keep the neck and shoulder muscles loose and relaxed...As you relax you'll notice how your breathing becomes easier and even seems to relax you...

Let's try the legs now. Tighten...Hold...now relax... let them hang freely. How good it feels when you're relaxed. Concentrate on that warm feeling in your toes and feet...feel that warmness as it spreads slowly to your legs and thighs... your hips...your shoulders...neck...Enjoy the pleasant feeling. Breathe slowly. Think about relaxing...relax your diaphragm...Just relax totally...Allow the feeling of relaxation to surround your body.

I'm going to count backwards and I want you to get even more relaxed: 10...you're very relaxed...9...you're more relaxed...8...The feeling is deeper...7...You feel so relaxed and comfortable...6...The relaxed feeling is spreading through every part of you now...5...Your breathing is slow, rhythmic, and deep...4...You can hear your body processes ...3...You feel so relaxed and comfortable...2...It's deeper and deeper...1...You're very deeply relaxed...and, oh, so calm...

I will soon count to three and you will return to your everyday state of consciousness...1...2...3...Now open your eyes.

SENSITIVITY TRAINING

Sensitivity training is a group process in which individuals are able to examine their feelings about themselves and others and are able to learn more about themselves based on feedback from the rest of the group. Unlike traditional therapy groups in which individuals examine traumatic experiences of the past, sensitivity training is oriented to the "here and now." The focus of the group is on how the members relate to one another and experience and resolve feelings of affection, conflict, and stress. The role of the leader, or facilitator, is to assist members in overcoming obstacles and to keep the group on-the-track.

Most of the other action techniques are self-directed—i.e., you can work through them on your own. Sensitivity training occurs in groups and adds the dimension of additional people to the process. This type of change strategy is most useful when your goals include the following:

1 Increasing your interpersonal sensitivity.

2 Learning honest and direct self-expression.

3 Encouraging and establishing more open relationships with other people.

While the research base of demonstrating any long-term behavior change is lacking, participants of sensitivity-training groups do report that something happens. New behaviors are tried out, new patterns of relating to people are emphasized, and intense emotional feelings are experienced. However, there is no reason to expect that these new behaviors and feelings will last, unless you establish a self-change program after the experience. Most likely, the sensitivity training will give you ideas for new goals. Any of the self-change strategies presented in this chapter can be selected, based on the appropriateness of the strategy for your goals, which can help facilitate long-term behavior change.

It is fairly easy to enroll in a sensitivity-training group as nearly all metropolitan areas throughout the United States offer such training. There are, however, dangers involved in enrolling in a sensitivity group. The success of your experience depends to a large extent on the qualifications of the group leader. Your best defense would be to carefully evaluate the credentials of the group leader before enrolling. This individual should be an experienced professional psychologist or psychiatrist or an experienced social worker or counselor.

ASSERTIVENESS TRAINING

Assertiveness training is a change strategy most often used when a person feels, "People seem to take advantage of me.... I don't know why....," or "Why can't I say no.... I didn't want to do it and here I am accepting the task." This method consists of arranging environmental situations so that the responses previously inhibited by anxiety can now be overtly expressed. The assertive behavior, or being able to express your true thoughts and feelings, that tends to replace the anxiety in the specified situations can result in positive consequences. Among the new feelings experienced are control and dominance.

One of the barriers to learning assertive behavior is that historically, behaving in such a manner has frequently resulted in punishment. For example, a mother tells her son to ignore his father when he is in a bad mood and try to understand him. Thus the child learns to suppress his legitimate feelings of wanting to defend himself. Not only does suppression occur at home, it occurs throughout our educational and job experiences, and in the limitations imposed by society on our relationships. No wonder that when our supervisor tells us off we have a difficult time standing up for ourselves.

For you to take advantage of assertiveness techniques, you need to identify and isolate specific target behaviors. You don't need to know *why* you are the way you are, you just need to know *what* you are doing. By answering the following questions, you should be able to focus on what you have to do to change.

1 In what kinds of situations do you find yourself being taken advantage of?

2 How do you feel when requests are made of you?

3 What do you typically say in response to requests?

4 What are the consequences of your behavior?

5 What do you have to do to change?

6 Refer to your answers to questions 1–5. Select one situation where you find yourself being taken advantage of and formulate an assertive response. Write the response in the space provided.

7 Finally, practice the response at home, at the office, in front of a mirror, etc., until you feel confident when using the assertive response.

Using the above format will give you a basic understanding of what you have to do to become assertive. If you should discover that the work you invested in the exercise does not help you, you may want to utilize the role-playing and/or modeling techniques which are presented later in this chapter.

PSYCHOTHERAPY

If you feel that you cannot adequately understand your problems and/or successfully complete your self-change program, you might consider seeking the assistance of a professionally-trained person. The inclusion of an individual, who is trained to help people change their behavior, may be all that you need to break through the barriers which have blocked your progress. The additional source of information, feedback, and insights can reduce the self-defeating experiences associated with your failure to successfully modify your behavior.

Qualified personnel who provide psychotherapy are licensed psychologists and psychiatrists, social workers, and counselors. In order for psychotherapy to be successful, it is necessary for you to recognize the *need* to change. Then the person you selected will be of help to you.

MODELING

It will be helpful for you in achieving your goal to observe the behavior of others who have successfully achieved the goal you have set for yourself. By carefully selecting and observing a *model* who has achieved the goals you want, you can absorb new ideas for your behavior. Actually, much of what we say and do is the result of imitative learning, or observing those around us before we respond to a situation. *Modeling*, then, is a strategy for learning by way of imitation.

Modeling can be used as a strategy for adding almost any new behavior you desire to your behavior repertoire. By observing how others assert themselves, you can generate ideas about how to be assertive. Other behaviors which may be learned by modeling are self-confidence, self-disclosure, openness, social manners, and behavior appropriate to sex role.

There are a variety of possible models to observe in your everyday environment. Most likely there is an individual, or *live model*, in your organization whom you respect and admire. In fact, you may have already picked up some of this individual's habits and methods of dealing with the problems of the job. When you observe the behavior of another person and learn new behaviors accordingly, you are following the live modeling strategy. Symbolic models, such as television and the movies, for example, are present in our lives as well.

In order to use the modeling strategy, it is necessary to have your goal identified. Then, you will know what to look for, how to be open to new approaches, and how to select appropriate models.

ROLE-PLAYING

Role-playing will enable you to gain an understanding of yourself and others in your organization, help you to determine how you may modify your behavior, and give you a chance to practice your newly-modified behavior. For role-playing to have its maximum effect, it should be performed under as realistic situations as possible, which means that you will probably need the assistance of a second person—someone you feel comfortable with and willing to participate in the process.

First we assign the roles. You will need to remember that the prerequisite of all change strategies is an accurate statement of the problem. This second person assumes the role of a significant person in your life—e.g., a manager, director, or supervisor—at the point where you want to change your behavior. Following a portrayal of the situation, analyze the dynamics.

Next we reverse roles, with the goal being to help you identify the thoughts, feelings, and attitudes of the other person. Finally we determine what you should do differently. The new behaviors are practiced until you are enough at ease with them to try them out in a real situation.

Role-playing could easily become a part of a multiple program of assertiveness training and/or modeling techniques. Role-playing offers you the added dimension of having another person in the process and gives you insight into how your new behavior may be viewed by another person in your organization.

BIBLIOTHERAPY

Bibliotherapy is the process of using books for therapeutic rather than instructional or leisure purposes. Books can provide a source of psychological relief from the pressures and concerns we face in our lives. You can use bibliotherapy to solve actual and existing problems and to relieve pressure or you can use it to cope with anticipated future problems.

The basic assumption of bibliotherapy is that when we read, we bring our own needs and problems to the reading experience. We interpret the author's words in light of our own experiences. By identifying with the characters in the book, we can develop a better understanding of ourselves.

Bibliotherapy incorporates three stages: (1) identification, (2) catharsis, and (3) insight. After you have selected a book and begun to read, the first thing that happens is that you begin to identify with a character in the book. As a result of the *identification*, you may experience a release of emotion or psychological tension—*catharsis*. Because of this release of tension, you are able to achieve additional *insight* into your problem.

There are two types of bibliotherapeutic literature. One type, consisting of fiction, biography, and inspirational literature, offers much in the way of varied expressions of human experience. The other type, consisting of literature on mental hygiene, provides useful information for solving human problems and covers practical principles and facts on adjustment problems. Much of this literature is referred to as self-help material.

Your reading of this book is an experience in bibliotherapy. Using this book will assist you in the development of your *Personal Development Strategy*, which will help you to meet your needs and realize your potential. The following is a list of books you may find useful in solving your problems. We have organized this representative list into three categories to aid your selection of material relevant to your concerns.

Awareness

    Otto, H., and J. Mann (ed.), *Ways of Growth*, New York: The Viking Press, 1968.

Stevens, J. O., *Awareness: Explaining, Experimenting, Experiencing,* Moab: Real People Press, 1971.

Assertive Behavior

Byrd, R. E., *A Guide to Personal Risk Taking,* New York: Amacon, 1974.

Alberti, R., and M. Emmons, *Your Perfect Right,* New York: Impact, 1974.

Smith, J. J., *When I Say No, I Feel Guilt,* New York: Dial Press, 1975.

Self-Improvement

Culbert, S. A., *The Organization Trap and How to Get Out of It,* New York: Basic Books, 1974.

Goodman, D., and M. Maultsby, *Emotional Well-Being Through Rational Behavior Training,* Springfield: Charles Thomas, 1974.

Langer, E. J., and C. S. Dweck, *Personal Politics: The Psychology of Making It,* Englewood Cliffs: Prentice-Hall, 1973.

Levitan, S. A., and W. B. Johnston, *Work Is Here to Stay, Alas,* Salt Lake City: Olympress, 1973.

Miller, S., E. Nunnally, and D. Wackman, *Alive and Aware: Improving Communication in Relationships,* Minneapolis: Interpersonal Communications Programs, 1975.

Newman, M., and B. Berkowitz, *How To Be Your Own Best Friend,* New York: Random House, 1971.

O'Neill, N., and G. O'Neill, *Shifting Gears,* New York: Avon Books, 1975.

Watson, D. L., and R. G. Thorp, *Self-Directed Behavior,* Monterey: Brooks/Cole, 1973.

RATIONAL BEHAVIOR TRAINING

David Goodman and Maxie Maultsby (1974) coined the term, *Rational Behavior Training,* in their recent book, *Emotional Well-Being Through Rational Behavior Training.* Rational Behavior Training (RBT) is a process of learning how to increase our reasoning skill so that we can better deal with the problems and crises of our daily living. It is based on the concept that our ability to reason enables us to keep our emotions under better control, which thereby enables us to see our problems clearly; problems can then be solved more effectively.

Basic to RBT is the concept of "self-talk," or "thought-language." Our emotions and behavior imply a content which is not expressed overtly but rather is expressed internally by everyone. Learning to analyze the thought process rationally and logically becomes the key to controlling and/or changing behavior. Through the use of "Rational Self-analysis," emotions lose their ambiguity and mystery, and we can assert control over our lives.

Rational Self-analysis, which is a written exercise containing four parts, is helpful whenever you experience an emotion you do not want. Use the following exercise to help prevent negative emotions.

1 Give a written description of the event which upset you. Stick to the facts; give no value judgments; and be objective.

2 What are your thoughts concerning the event? State your subjective value judgments, your biases, and what you think is appropriate.

3 Identify and label your emotional responses. *Remember:* use a one-word label for an emotion—e.g., love, anger, sadness—not a phrase, such as "I was hurt because I did not get the promotion," as this statement contains both a thought (which belongs in Part 1) and a feeling.

4 Take your subjective, irrational statements from Part 2 and correct them. Look for statements of absolutes, being perfect, and being right. Rationally challenge these statements and correct faulty judgments to make them more reasonable.

THOUGHT STOPPING

Many people sometimes are so obsessed with an idea that they "can't get it out of their mind." Usually, it concerns something dreadful, terrible, catastrophic, or horrible; for example, "I'm going to be fired," or "Someone is going to discover how incompetent I really am," or "My family is going to leave me." The necessity of thought-stopping should be obvious, as it enables a person to get rid of irrational thoughts.

The process works like this: Visualize yourself in a scene in which some awful event is about to occur. When you have developed it, shout, "Stop!" and then replace the image with a pleasant scene. Repeat the process with different scenes. After practicing the image switch, you will become adept at shifting from unpleasant feelings to pleasant feelings.

IMPLEMENTING YOUR SELF-CHANGE STRATEGY— THE CASE OF RON AND JANET SAMUELS

Our main concern is facilitating your process of making major life decisions and changes. At this stage of your development, you have assessed your developmental tasks, identified your primary needs and values, determined your personality style, and examined how well they fit your organization's needs and values. As a result, you have decided that you are dissatisfied wtih your current behavior and that you need to develop a self-change program. The remainder of this chapter describes how you can do it!

The Ron Samuels' case gives a good example of how to go about changing yourself. As you recall, Ron determined that the primary developmental task confronting him was a questioning of his marriage and his relationship with his wife. Though the process could be painful for him, he discovered that in order to develop further, he would have to resolve this task.

The next step in his self-assessment involved identifying his primary values, which were rank-ordered as follows:

Ranked values	Weights
Physical:	
1. Comfort	5
2. Attractiveness	3
(cont.)	

Ranked values	Weights
Emotional:	
1. Security/Family	5
2. Prestige	4
Intellectual:	
1. Wisdom	4
2. Reading	2

After completing the value-clarification exercise, Ron looked at his dominant personality style; the controller/Right-One aspects of his personality were identified in the process. At this point, Ron was beginning to get a clear picture of how he was contributing to his marital problems.

We will assume that Ron completed the assessment of his marriage as described in Chapter 6. From this assessment and based on his experiences in the marriage/organization, Ron now needs to determine his fit in the marriage. The first step in the process is for him to assign weights to his rank-ordered values as he perceives how other members of the organization/marriage would weight them, given their understanding of Ron's needs and values. Ron's perceptions looked like this:

Ranking-order (Ron)	Weights (organization)
Physical:	
1. Comfort	5
2. Attractiveness	2
Emotional:	
1. Security/Family	5
2. Prestige	3
Intellectual:	
1. Wisdom	2
2. Reading	1

The area of conflict occurs between Ron's high weighting of intellectual activities and the organization's low weighting of his intellectual needs. However, there seems to be a fairly close match in the other two value areas. The next step is for Ron to develop the Match-mismatch Index by multiplying the weights by each other. The results were as follows:

Values	Weights				Match-mismatch total
	Ron	×	Organization		
Physical:					
Comfort	5	×	5	=	25
Attractiveness	3	×	2	=	6
Emotional:					
Security/Family	5	×	5	=	25
Prestige	4	×	3	=	12
Intellectual:					
Wisdom	4	×	2	=	8
Reading	2	×	1	=	2

The Match-mismatch Index shows the difficulty Ron was experiencing in the intellectual domain, as he had already suspected. However, Ron discovered that there was mutual concern for comfort and family security. Ron began to realize that being away from home for extended periods was in conflict with his family/security values. He was making a good salary, but his family life was deteriorating. He began to feel that some of the problems he was experiencing resulted from his insistence that Janet value the same intellectual pursuits that he did. This was the reason he felt embarrassed around his college-educated colleagues. Janet just couldn't match up to *his* expectations.

Ron now had to use the Match-mismatch Index to decide what he should do. His completed decision-making grid, in which he incorporated the Match-mismatch Index, follows:

Values		Alternatives			
Ranked values	Match-mismatch index	Leave	Stay the same	Change self	Change organization
Physical:					
Comfort	25	+ (25)	−− (−50)	++ (50)	+ (25)
Attractiveness	6	0 (0)	0 (0)	0 (0)	0 (0)
Emotional:					
Security/Family	25	−− (−50)	++ (50)	++ (50)	− (−25)
Prestige	12	+ (12)	−− (−24)	− (−12)	+ (12)
Intellectual:					
Wisdom	8	++ (8)	− (−8)	++ (16)	++ (16)
Reading	2	++ (2)	0 (0)	++ (4)	++ (2)
Totals		−3	−32	+108	+30

The results of the decision-making grid confirmed what Ron had begun to suspect; he had to do something about *his* behavior, and try to understand what was important to Janet and what her needs were. He needed to realign some of his priorities. However, he also discovered that changing his marriage was also a viable choice. What Ron did decide was that he would develop a self-change program, evaluate its success, and, if necessary, involve Janet in trying to change their marriage/organization, if his self-modification program did not succeed.

Ron had two final tasks to perform: (1) select an appropriate change strategy and (2) develop and implement the program. Based on his personality assessment, Ron found that his problem concerned being inflexible and rigid (Right One) and a need to exercise power through controlling his wife and not showing his feelings (Controller). Referring to the "Guide for Selecting Self-Change Strategies" presented in Chapter 5, Ron looked under the problem heading, found where he fit, and then compared the different change strategies that were available to him. After studying the descriptions of each strategy, he decided that he would enroll in a sensitivity-training group. That fit in with an opportunity at work in which the company was sponsoring a week-long sensitivity-training course for its regional managers. Ron figured that he could "kill two birds with one stone."

The final step was for Ron to develop his *Implementation-Evaluation* program. He needed to establish a format which would provide him with a detailed plan of action and a feedback mechanism so that he could check his progress. Ron developed the following plan.

SPECIFIC GOALS FOR CHANGE

Ron's specific goal was to save his marriage. He had diagnosed his problem as a lack of concern and respect for his wife's needs. He had not taken her needs into consideration when he suggested that she read certain material nor had he spent the necessary time at home to assist her in raising the children. He needed to modify his attentiveness and listening ability so that Janet could begin to develop her potential in the direction *she* perferred. Specifically, Ron's goals were:

1 To change his response patterns so that Janet could express her needs and concerns.

2 To improve the communication pattern between himself and Janet from a direction-power orientation to collaborative-person orientation.

3 To reassign his time commitments so as to allow himself more opportunity for family involvement.

OPERATIONALIZING THE GOAL

Ron knew how to change; now he had to convert his goals into measurable and observable dimensions. Specifically, he needed to specify *what* he had to do, *when* it was to be done, and *how* he would know *when* he had accomplished his goals. Ron developed the following list to help him put his plan in action.

1 I will enroll in the company-sponsored sensitivity-training group, which begins on February 15 and will be completed on February 20.

2 I will attend all sessions, participate fully in all lectures, demonstrations, and exercises, and practice listening skills during the training sessions.

3 On the first Friday evening I am home, I will practice my listening skills with Janet to determine what her needs and values are.

4 Whenever Janet and I are discussing ways to make our lives happier, I will take every opportunity to practice responding to her and will contribute my ideas as well.

5 I will increase the time I spend at home by five hours per week.

6 In order to determine whether my strategy has worked, I will actively solicit feedback from Janet and will monitor my feelings for her when we are with my friends.

ESTABLISHING SUBGOALS

Ron developed a series of substeps as he felt that achieving these smaller steps would reinforce and help maintain his motivation. Specifically, he stated:

1 I will submit my request for enrollment in the sensitivity-training group in writing to my supervisor in two days.
2 I will announce to each member of my training group what I hope to learn during the week.
3 I will share with Janet my objectives in attending the training group and my new time schedule.
4 I will brainstorm with Janet to develop a list of her priorities and needs, upon completion of the training session.

BUILDING IN REWARDS

Ron felt that there were several pay-offs for changing his behavior. He certainly was not receiving any positive reaction from Janet for his suggestions on how she could change and what she should do. He felt that if he could understand her needs from her frame of reference, he could get to know her better and recognize her potential and attributes. He didn't really understand how Janet could cope with the stress of raising the children and remain content in her role. As he involved himself more in the family, the children began to respond more favorably to him. He then began to feel like part of the family and not like an outsider as he had for the past two years.

Ron felt that not only would he feel better, but the atmosphere at home would be less tense. Also, his feelings of embarrassment at social gatherings began to cease as he started to see Janet as more than someone to put on display to bring him recognition.

CHECK POINTS

Ron established several check points to ensure the proper implementation of his program; among them were:

1. Follow-up on my request to my supervisor by personally contacting him.
2. Clear my calendar of obligations for the week of the sensitivity-training group sessions.
3. Solicit written feedback from group members.
4. Report to Janet what I learned and what she can expect.
5. Keep a record of the number of hours per week I am spending with my family.

Ron realized that his plan would take a great deal of effort. He felt his choice of alternatives was his best hope of relieving feelings of dissatisfaction and helping him through the reassessment of his marriage. Ron felt that when he had completed the program he would have a happier marriage.

Chapter 10
Strategies for Organizational Change

Joe Brennon's Match-mismatch Index indicated wide discrepancies between his personal needs and values and those of his organization. Such a low Match-mismatch Index suggests that, if Joe continues in his present situation, the dissatisfaction currently being experienced by him and his organization would probably be intensified. Completion of the Person/Organization-match Decision-making Grid in Chapter 7 led us to the conclusion that Joe's best informed decision would be to resign his job. His next highest-weighted course of action would be to change the organization.

If you should determine that you are in a position similar to Joe Brennon's, where family and personal needs are tied to the local community, then you may decide to change the organization to make it more compatible with your needs. Although this strategy will require a lot of personal energy, it will be worth the effort if you feel that there is a reasonable chance of it being successful. If you are not successful, the alternative of resignation is still available.

If you decide to invest your effort in making your organization's values more compatible with your own, it is important that you perceive the organization, not as a fixed external structure with set rules, powers, and goals, but as a perceived social reality within which individuals can make decisions. Shifting our personal frame of reference will give us a different perspective of the organization —that is, from a "fixed-given" view, which we can only respond to, to an "agreed-upon social-invention" view, which members of the organization have created and now take for granted. In this view, individuals not only create the organization, but they "are" the organization; thus we can change the organization by changing the perceptions, awareness, and values of those involved in it.

Before we discuss specific techniques for changing the organization, we should understand the role of the successful inside change agent—that is, how you should behave to optimize your chances for bringing about desired changes. You should also be familiar with the considerations necessary for reducing resistance to change and increasing chances of success for all change strategies. Finally, you should be aware of what to consider when selecting an appropriate change strategy.

ROLE OF AN INSIDE CHANGE AGENT

Ronald Havelock (1973) of the University of Michigan Institute for Social Research has combined the experience of researchers and practicing change agents in an analysis of over 1000 studies of innovation and the process of change. Although aimed primarily at educational organizations, the material revealed in his book, *The Change Agent's Guide to Innovation in Education*, is highly applicable to all types of organizations and forms the basis for much of this chapter. Havelock's findings concerning the relative advantages of being either an "insider" or "outsider" appear to be a good place to start when considering your role as an "inside" change agent.

Advantages and Disadvantages of the "Inside" Change Agent

Although outside change agents possess several advantages (such as being independent and having an objective, new perspective), they also have several disadvantages (such as being a stranger, lacking "inside" understanding, and not being able to identify adequately with problems). As insiders, we are more intimately concerned about the welfare of our organization and our own well-being, which gives us a motivation different from that of monetary compensation for initiating change processes.

The following are some of the *advantages* of being an inside change agent:

1 *You know the system.* You know where the power is, who the opinion leaders are, where the strategic leverage points are.
2 *You understand and speak the language of the organization.* The special ways members refer to things and the tone and style of discussing things are familiar to you.
3 *You understand the norms.* You probably follow and behave in accordance with commonly held beliefs, attitudes, and behaviors.
4 *You identify with the organization's needs and goals.* If the organization prospers, this will probably benefit you, thus you have a personal incentive for contributing.
5 *You are a familiar figure.* What you are trying to do will be understandable as "member" behavior; you don't represent the threat of an unfamiliar outside force.

As an insider, however, you also have the following *disadvantages:*

1 *You may lack an "objective" perspective.* Because of your involvement and history with the organization, you may be biased or not be able to see the organization as a whole system.
2 *You may not have the special knowledge or skill required.* Since consulting is not your primary vocation, you may not have had enough training to be regarded as a true expert in the change situation.
3 *You may not have an adequate power base.* Unless you are in a position of authority in organization, you may be confronted by superiors or competing peers when you present your plans.
4 *You may be hindered by past images.* You may have to live down past failures or the hostility generated by past successes.
5 *You may not have independence of movement required to be effective.* The obligations of your job may severely limit the time and energy that you can invest in a change-agent role.
6 *It may be difficult to redefine your on-going relationships with other members of the organization.* When taking on the

change-agent role, you must be able to change the expectations that your associates have about how you will behave and how they will relate to you.

Many experienced professionals have suggested that, in order to capitalize on the advantages and avoid the disadvantages of being an inside change agent, insiders work with outsiders as a team. Such a team would provide the insider with "expert" legitimacy for his efforts, expertise, an objective perspective, and moral support. For most of us who wish to act as inside change agents, however, the contacts and wherewithal for obtaining the outside half of our team are missing. Nevertheless, there are some commonly accepted principles which can help us to reduce the disadvantages and capitalize on the advantages of being an insider.

Ten Principles of Being a Successful Inside Change Agent

Even though you do not have the advantage of outside support and are not in a position of authority within your organization, it is, nevertheless, possible to be effective in bringing about change. There are some generally accepted principles which can help you to work successfully from within and below. These principles, which should be kept in mind in all change situations and are prerequisites to any specific change technique, are as follows.

Know yourself To bring about desired changes, it is first necessary to truly *know yourself*. We must be aware of our needs, values, and objectives in order to determine what it is that we need to be happy in our organization. If we react to what current fads indicate is desirable or to others' expectations, we may be successful in gaining social approval, but fail to satisfy our own specific needs. We may or may not desire what is "right" for others, or what others think we should want. Completing your Personal Development Strategy and Person/Organization Match Index is our suggested method for getting to know yourself.

Understand the organization If our change strategies are to be effective, we must truly *understand the organization*. Knowledge of values, norms, key people, subsystems, cliques and alliances is prerequisite for assessing the situation and planning realistic change efforts. After completing the Organization Assessment Exercise in Chapter 6, you should have a pretty good understanding of the nature of your organization's values and processes. Your personal history can serve as a basis for understanding various cliques and alliances, and your personal knowledge can be supplemented through contacts with "political" colleagues.

Keep lines of communication open In order to make informed decisions, we must *keep the lines of communication open*. One of the most devastating blockages to change efforts occurs when we cut off communications with our adversaries, which can cause an affirmation of negative stereotypes without the possibility of new disconfirming information that could shed new light on the situation. This is what happened to Dick Larsen when he failed to communicate his concern to his supervisor and perceived competitor. Had he shared information about his feelings, he might have received feedback which would have served to disconfirm his negative assumptions and would have allowed him to avoid behavior which led to his current predicament.

Determine how others feel It is important to *determine how others feel* about a situation and whether or not they agree with your desires. If no one else agrees with your assessment of the situation, maybe another *self*-assessment is called for. On the other hand, if you can identify potential allies who share your desires, they can contribute to an effective team effort that has a high probability of success. If Joe Brennon, for example, had asked around and found that he was the only person dissatisfied with the university's assessment system, he would probably have little luck finding support for changes in the directions he desires.

Analyze the different points of view The situation should be *analyzed from the many points of view* of all parties involved. Assessing the perceptions of a proposed change from adversaries' points of view may reveal how they might have overlooked an important point that would have changed their minds. It might, on the other hand, demonstrate something that convinces you to alter your position. In Joe Brennon's case, gaining insight into how the senior faculty perceive important links with the business community as vital to maintaining research support contributions may help him understand why they think it is important for all faculty members to present a physical image that meets with businessmen's expectations of how a "responsible" professor should look.

Understand all dimensions thoroughly A *thorough understanding* of all dimensions of the proposed change is a prerequisite. You, as the innovator, must be "the expert" in the change situation in order to maintain your own credibility and to aid others in understanding what you are trying to bring about. Your knowledge should include all strengths, weaknesses, evaluations, and possible objections. If Joe Brennon hopes to succeed in changing the minds of senior faculty to allow for more personal expression in appearance, it would behoove him to first survey the business community and obtain evidence that it now recognizes creativity and competence as the primary criteria for distributing research fund contributions.

Continue the effort Successful change is not usually accomplished without *continued effort*. The innovator must be persistent and continually make inroads whenever opportunities present themselves. Giving up before you start leads to very predictable negative results. The most extreme type of failure in adhering to this principle was demonstrated by Dick Larsen, who gave up and resigned before spending any effort to improve the situation. In the case of Ron Samuels, if the marriage organization is to survive, both parties must be committed to continued efforts to improve it.

Have a sense of timing A sense of *timing* is just as important as the strategy employed. Waiting for the opportune moment, as opposed to reacting spontaneously, can make a key difference in the success of a change effort. But even the most elaborate strategies may fail to be effective unless political and environmental forces are in your favor. Waiting too long for the right moment can, however, force more negative developments. If Joe Brennon had assessed the values of senior faculty earlier, for example, he might have had adequate time to convince them to alter their opinions, or to alter his appearance if he found their reasons justified, before the crucial decision was made. Now that the ax has fallen, his job will be more difficult.

Share the credit *Sharing credit* with others can also be vital in creating enthusiasm about a desired change. People support and feel committed to ideas they feel a part of. The pleasure you feel when have done something for yourself is much greater than that you feel when you are benefiting from someone else's change. This idea of joint effort is a key factor in the Samuels's case. If Ron and Janet can jointly assess their situation and together develop change strategies, the chances of their success will be much greater than if Ron tries to force his ideas of what's best for Janet to do on her.

Avoid win-lose strategies *Avoiding win-lose strategies* and seeking changes where everybody wins can help prevent standoffs, where everyone loses what they want directly or indirectly because of hard feelings. Cooperative win-win changes enhance the positions of all parties involved and contribute to long-run benefits. Win-lose strategies may get you what you want in the short-run, if you have the power and luck needed to bring it about. However, your adversaries will be waiting to deal with you, without consideration of your needs in future controversies, just as you dealt with them in the past. If Dick Larsen had been able to perceive his situation as one where both he and Wilfred could win, he might have avoided having to make a decision where both he and the company lost.

Defining Your Role as an Inside Change Agent

Regardless of your formal job title or position, there are four primary ways in which a person can act as a change agent. These roles have been defined by Ronald Havelock (1973) as the following:

1 *Catalyst* The Catalyst's role is needed to overcome existing inertia and start the organization members working on their serious problems. As we discussed earlier, most people usually want to keep things the way they are and, consequently, resist change. A Catalyst's role is natural for someone who has completed his or her Personal Development Strategy and has decided to attempt to change the organization because its primary requirement is to make personal dissatisfaction known. By upsetting the status quo catalysts energize the problem-solving process.

2 *Solution Giver* As a Solution Giver you will have the opportunity to present your ideas about what the organizational change should be. In order to have your suggestions accepted, however, you must know when and how to offer them, and how others in the organization can adapt them to their needs.

3 *Process Helper* This is a critical role concerning the "how to" or process of change. It involves showing organizational members how to (a) recognize and define their needs; (b) diagnose problems and set objectives, (c) acquire relevant resources; (d) select or create solutions; (e) adapt and carry out solutions; and (f) evaluate solutions.

4 *Resource Linker* The Resource Linker brings people and resources together so that they can be applied to the problem. Resources include people with necessary skills and knowledge as well as with financial and political backing.

In defining your role, keep in mind that all of these roles are necessary and you may be able to fill more than one of them yourself. In other words, the roles are not mutually exclusive. Just because you are a Catalyst does not mean that you can't also serve as a Solution Giver, Process Helper, or Resource Linker as well. It is also possible for you to be effective in these change roles regardless of whether you are "line" or "staff," or working from above or below. It is often difficult to bring about change when you do not have formal power, but it can be done, especially when you apply the ten principles previously outlined.

Tips for Being Successful in Each Change Agent Role

All four change-agent roles are important and interrelated. The principal tasks of a change agent are to establish and build a relationship with the organizational members he wishes to change, to work with them collaboratively in a problem-solving process, and to leave them with the ability to solve similar problems effectively for themselves in the future. Requirements for different roles often occur simultaneously; but regardless of when they are needed or who fulfills them, each role deserves consideration at every phase of a change effort.

How to be an effective Catalyst A Catalyst is an initial change advocate who stresses the need for change to further either the interests of the organization or of disadvantaged subgroups and individuals. Catalysts are often deeply committed to and emotionally involved in the change effort because they personally feel injured, or because they identify with some subgroup which they feel is being exploited. To maximize their effectiveness as emotionally-involved change advocates, Catalysts need to make certain that they do the following:

1 Think reasonably about steps that need to be taken to win support for their cause and to reduce resistance to the changes they desire.

2 Try to see the situation from the point of view of the existing organizational leaders. This is often difficult, but it lets the Catalysts know when and how to be effective influencers so that they have better chances of success when they confront organizational leaders to win their support.

3 Promote a feeling of common identity and purpose in those supporting the change effort.

4 Form alliances with others who can take on other change-agent roles, such as Process Helper or Resource Linker. The Catalyst may be seen as a troublemaker or a disrupter. Though he may be able to overcome this perception, the change effort will probably be more effective if it is the result of teamwork and collaboration.

5 Have a sense of timing. Catalysts need to assess support for the change and select the most opportune moment for bringing it about. Even if they are "hot" on issues, Catalysts can not be successful if there are few symptoms of unrest and no voices of protest but their own. Organizations in stable equilibrium are unlikely to be changed by the acts of a single individual. Organizations undergoing crisis and facing a number of disruptive elements, on the other hand, are more likely to be susceptible to change efforts.

How to be an effective Solution Giver Most of us have, at one time or another, thought that we had a better solution to an organizational problem than the one adopted; and, a large percentage of the time, we probably did. Whether or not we were an effective "Solution Giver," however, depends on how well we communicated our solution to others. People have a tendency to become notoriously obstinate if they think someone is trying to "sell" them something. Consequently, as Solution Givers, we need to concentrate on the following check points:

1 Unearth the real goals of the organization before you decide that it needs the solution you have in mind.
2 Adapt innovations so that they are maximally beneficial to all members of the organization.
3 Have more than one solution available and keep them flexible.
4 Ensure that those who will be affected by the change will continue to assist after the change has been adopted.
5 Help the organizational decision-makers judge the solutions so that they can decide for themselves what is best for all.
6 Build an open and authentic relationship with others in the organization by knowledge-sharing and helping.
7 Become a resource linker to aid the organization in implementing the solution.

How to be an effective Resource Linker Most of us have difficulty asking for and giving help. Problem-solving, however, is largely a process of matching one person's or group's resources with the needs of another. Consequently, people with skills in communicating and relationship-building are important change agents in the Resource-Linker role. To be most effective Resource Linkers should do the following:

1 Listen to what the organizational leaders have to say about their problems and what they have done to solve them. Resource Linkers must understand "where the organization is at" before they can successfully match its needs with the right kind of resource, at the right time, in the right way.
2 Establish two-way communication between the Resource Linkers and the organizations. This may be an awkward or clumsy

process at first, but it is the only way an effective helping relationship can be built.

3 Show organizational leaders the resources they have within themselves and among the members of their group, as well as outside resources. Effective problem-solving over time requires multiple exchanges between inside and outside Resource Linkers, each representing special knowledge and skills relevant to different needs at different times.

4 Continue building additional networks after the initial problem has been resolved. Each new resource link established adds to the organization's capacity to work collaboratively on problems.

How to be an effective Process Helper The helping process is necessary from the beginning stages of establishing a relationship and diagnosing a problem, through to the stages of acquisition of relevant resources, choosing a solution, gaining acceptance, and stabilizing the change. There are important process factors to be considered at each stage of the change effort which can facilitate its success. Three things necessary to building and maintaining an effective Process-Helper relationship with the change target (individual, group, or total organization) are as follows:

1 *Definition of your relationship with the organization.* If you know where you stand and how others see you, you will be in a better position to adapt to and enhance the relationship and change effort. You will need to know (1) "What is the nature of the group you will work directly with?" and (2) "What are the groups to which the target group is related?"

After you have determined the target group you will be working with, it will be helpful to understand its nature—not only the norms, values, and beliefs of this group, but also how strictly they are adhered to. To determine who can best facilitate your efforts, you need to determine the formal and the "informal" key people or "opinion leaders" to whom others turn for new ideas. These "gatekeepers" hold key positions with respect to the flow of new ideas and information. After you have assessed the situation you will be in a position to determine who it would be best to work with—opinion leaders, formal authorities, or representatives of major factions; who has credibility, respectability, or public-relations ability; and who is compatible with you. These are key considerations in making these decisions.

In answer to the second basic question "What are the other groups to whom the target group is related?", we need to analyze the surrounding environment. This may be either the organization, if you are working with a subgroup, or the community if you are working with the organization as the group. To aid your understanding of the surrounding environment, you should determine what norms, values, and objectives and the degree of influence it has for the target group. It is also important to determine the relative potency of different influences in the larger environment—i.e., pressure groups, individuals, and institutions, if they are together or factional or conservative, and how these influences can best be approached.

2 *Successful management of initial encounters with the target group.* How those in the target group see you and feel about you will initially determine whether or not you will be able to proceed with the change process at all. In your initial encounter with the target group, remember to be friendly, informed about their situation, helpful, and responsive. Being viewed as an intruder, the change agent must begin the relationship by establishing trust and friendliness. Simple things—like smiling, a firm handshake, a warm greeting, a direct look in the eye, or using first names—will start you in the right direction. Appropriate dress, speech, bearing, and common interests will also be helpful. Effective change agents are usually similar to target group members in many respects, or at least they are perceived to be that way.

In order to establish a cooperative image, find something you can do for the change target that will be perceived as being helpful. Only a "token" offering is usually necessary, such as providing a useful piece of information, a book, or explaining a technique. Finally, show that you are a good listener, that you are interested, and that you care. This can be communicated by asking for clarification, nodding, paraphrasing, and other verbal and nonverbal techniques.

3 *Accurate assessment of your relationship.* A healthy relationship with the change target is the key to successful planned change. Since all situations are different, there is no set of specific criteria that "fit" all circumstances. There are, however, several characteristics of an "ideal" relationship which you can compare with your own situation. There are also some "danger signals," which will tip you off to negative conditions.

Ronald Havelock (1973) has identified nine characteristics of a change agent's relationship with a target group that comprise an ideal situation; they can serve as a yardstick against which we can measure our own circumstances. An ideal relationship includes the following:

1 *Reciprocity.* Both the change agent and target group should be able to transfer (give and take) information both ways and should mutually appreciate the problem.
2 *Openness.* Both should be willing to receive new inputs from each other.
3 *Realistic expectations.* Reasonably realistic expectations should be set from the start so that the change effort will not be plagued by undue disillusionment.
4 *Expectations of reward.* The change agent should be seen as a valuable resource who can solve problems and significantly improve the situation.
5 *Structure.* Definition of roles, working procedures, and expected outcomes is necessary to provide a sufficient structural basis for successful interactions.
6 *Equal power.* Under most circumstances, lasting effectiveness and commitment can best be brought about where neither party has the power to compel the other to change. Where there is an unequal distribution of power, usually only the "appearance" of change occurs by the seeming compliance of the weaker party.

7 *Minimum threat.* Because the idea of change is threatening to most of us, everything possible should be done to minimize the perception of threat.

8 *Confrontation of differences.* A relationship which allows an honest confrontation and the discussion of differences may be stormy at times, but it will also be healthy and strong when the going gets rough.

9 *Involvement of all relevant parties.* As noted earlier, as a change agent you should be able to relate to influential members of the community, who should at least know that you are there, why you are there, and approve of your being there.

A change effort can be an exciting and rewarding experience for everyone involved; however, it can also degenerate into a meaningless exercise of frustration and disappointment. Some "danger signals" which could warn you of a potentially bad relationship and the probable failure of your change effort, can be identified by careful analysis on your part. Some examples follow.

If the organization has persistently been indifferent to accepting innovation, there may be little point in trying to help it change. The organization may already be committed to a position leaving little opportunity for real innovation. This is also true if the target group is powerless or if it is completely dominated by leaders who are fundamentally hostile to change. Finally, if the key members of the organization lack the ability to assemble resources, communicate, or exhibit concern, or if the organization seems to be excessively rigid and tends to externalize conflicts, viewing issues only in terms of black-and-white, it could signify an innate inability to change.

Even if these degenerative organizational conditions do not exist, you as a change agent could do everything right and still be greeted with hostility or indifference. Negative responses to a well-managed initial-encounter effort may indicate that the future is not very bright. If you are greeted in an overly enthusiastic manner, on the other hand, the organizational leaders may want to use you as a pawn. This is a common type of exploitation where the change agent is supported only to serve special interests in an internal power struggle. A change agent may in rare instances be able to turn this type of situation to his advantage, but in general it should be avoided.

CONSIDERATIONS IN CHOOSING A CHANGE STRATEGY

It is important that anyone desiring to bring about a change first develop strategies to fit his own unique characteristics and circumstances. The strategies discussed in the following sections may provide useful ideas, but it is your own experience, level of competence, and overall objectives which are most important in developing a game plan. Some general considerations, which should always be a part of your strategy building, are listed below.

Personal Skill and Style

As a change agent you should have a realistic understanding of your own skills and best styles. The tactics discussed below should be applied in an appropriate way in appropriate situations. Misapplication of a good tactic may actually cause the situation to deteriorate even further. Stick with techniques that you know are applicable and that you are competent to administer. As an aid in making an appropriate strategy mix work, capitalize on your and the organization's resources, which include internal, external, human, material, informational, and motivational resources.

Type of Relationship

Political and economic tensions must also be considered when picking a strategy. If you are regarded as an expert and if people have confidence in you, the number and types of tactics which will be acceptable are greater than if you are considered a peer or novice.

Special Characteristics of the Organization

One of your first steps as a change agent is to make a thorough assessment of the organization to understand its strengths, weaknesses, ideologies, structural characteristics, and other special features. These considerations should then be carefully weighed to determine appropriate strategies—A strategy which does not fit the situation will do more harm than good. Specific situational factors, such as time, place, and circumstance, can provide restraints as well as guides to appropriate strategies.

Characteristics of the Strategy

The strategy must also be analyzed in relationship to the organization to determine the following: Is the strategy compatible with organizational ideologies? How much adaptation will be required to "make it fit" this situation? What is the probability of its success? How long will it be before the results become apparent? How much can be accomplished? How much effort will be required? By whom? For how long?

Feasibility

When evaluating competing strategies you should determine the following: How much benefit would it provide if it works? Will it work, especially in this particular organization? Will it be accepted by members of the organization? Asking these questions and comparing your answers for each strategy will often reduce the number of possible approaches to one or two.

Implementation

When you start planning how to implement the particular strategy or strategy mix you have decided upon, the relevance of the above criteria will become immediately apparent. If you do not possess adequate skills, have not established an appropriate relationship, or have failed to consider a value conflict between the organization and strategy-mix characteristics, the infeasibility of your proposed strategy will become clear when you try to implement it. Hopefully, you can avoid disaster at this stage if you will double check the feasibility of your change program by developing an implementation plan.

Your implementation plan for your organizational change strategy can follow the one provided in Chapter 8 for implementing and evaluating your Personal Development Strategy. The parallel steps for your organizational change strategy are as follows:

1 State specific goals for change.
2 Operationalize these goals—i.e., determine who will do what, when, where, and how.
3 Set up subgoals and substrategies to facilitate your primary objective.
4 Build in reward systems to ensure payoffs for cooperation in your program.
5 Set up check points to provide you with timely feedback about the progress of the change effort.

In the following two sections, we will summarize a wide range of organizational change strategies. The first section includes behavioral skills that we can utilize in developing our personal style of influencing others. The strategies presented in the second section are more complex. They can be used if you are an experienced facilitator or have an expert available to assist with the change effort. The strategies presented in both sections should be screened according to the above criteria and applied according to our suggested guidelines.

INTERPERSONAL STRATEGIES FOR ORGANIZATION CHANGE

This section presents behavioral skills that you can apply to cause change in others' behavior and attitudes. You may already be using some of the strategies we propose in interpersonal situations; we will show you how to increase their effectiveness. Other strategies relate to behaviors you have probably never examined, and may require practice before you feel comfortable with them. We present these interpersonal techniques to raise your awareness of different approaches for increasing your personal control over situations through effective communication and utilization of your own and others' resources.

Although the following list does not include all possible strategies it does give you some basics and it may provide you with insights which will give you the extra personal power required to effectively bring about the changes you desire. These strategies may also stimulate ideas and alternatives that are unique to your situation and personality style. You must choose your strategy in accordance with your special circumstances. The results of your personal and organizational assessments and the development of your Personal Development Strategy can provide key inputs in the development of your eclectic set of tactics, congruent with your unique experience, personality, and situation.

Some of the interpersonal change strategies you may want to consider are summarized below. For a more thorough explanation of these and similar strategies, you may wish to consult the books by Richard Byrd, Samuel Culbert, Ronald Havelock, and Ellen Langer and Carol Dweck, which are referenced at the end of this chapter.

Directed Thinking

Just as our Personal Development Strategy provides us with a game plan for guiding our lives, directed thinking can help us guide our behavior in interpersonal situations in ways which will result in our intended consequences. Directed thinking requires that you clearly specify what it is you hope to accomplish in an interpersonal situation and systematically consider all the factors which may influence your achieving it. Spontaneity is helpful in building strong interpersonal relationships, but it can hurt people. When we hurt or insult others without thinking, it often is very difficult to undo the damage; sometimes the damage is irreparable. Directed thinking will give you the foresight to prevent such a situation in the first place.

There is an abundance of information available to help guide your behavior in a directed way in any interpersonal situation. The following questions will help you select and organize this information in a meaningful way. How has this person or group reacted in similar situations? What approaches have worked in the past? Which approaches did not work? How does this person or group feel about me? How can I influence this impression? How does this person or group feel about the change being proposed? What is their point of view? Why? What is the most effective way of communicating the change ideas? What unique considerations are relevant to this person or group in this situation?

Disclaimers

The way in which we interact with others greatly influences their reactions. If the target person or group feels that you will personally benefit from the change you are suggesting, they may feel that they are being "ripped off" for your personal gain, or that you are unduly biased. To counter this attitude, you should "disclaim" these suppositions. If you will benefit from the change, you should admit it; but you should also attempt to convince the target person or group that the change will be a good thing for them regardless of your situation. By acknowledging your situation (which they may be aware of anyway), the target person or group may be disarmed by your sincerity in leveling with them. They can then listen to what you have to say without constantly being on guard against the unexpected.

If you are emotionally involved in the situation you are trying to change, your credibility may be reduced even if you make a disclaimer. This will especially be true if you only present the positive effects of the proposed change, as this may lead people to discredit your objectivity and judgment. In such circumstances it sometimes helps to present a more balanced account of the situation and strategies you are suggesting. This approach is more likely to convince others that you have thoroughly investigated the situation, regardless of your emotional concerns.

Authentic Feedback: Leveling

Authentic feedback is a nonevaluative interpretation of how a person's or group's behavior affects you. It often leads to the target person's or group's increased understanding of problems that their behavior creates. Such self-diagnosis decreases resistance to change especially when the personal need for it is demonstrated and accepted.

Sometimes leveling is done in an emotional or evaluative manner. Such confrontations are risky, but sometimes necessary for bringing out hidden feelings and opening doors to suppressed organizational problems. Confrontation is certainly better than suppression of hostile feelings, which may later be transferred to inappropriate people or circumstances.

Initial Agreement

It is important that you be agreeable with the target person or group when you begin your change effort, to ensure that you will not be "turned off" immediately. Discussing interests you have in common with the target person or group will favorably dispose them toward you and your proposal. Even if you should contradict yourself or propose contrary approaches at a later date, if the target person or group believes that you are similar to them, then they will be more responsive to your ideas.

Inoculation

If you feel that the target person or group, or other influential people, will later attempt to refute your position, it may be a good idea to inoculate the key decision-makers against arguments which could cause them to change their minds. This can often be done by sharing possible counterarguments with the target person or group and demonstrating their fallacies during your presentation. Using this technique tends to build up resistance to any opposition that may later be voiced.

Limited Choice

Most people like to feel that they have some control over what happens to them, but when faced with an unlimited number of alternatives from which to choose, it becomes very difficult to make a decision. Having a limited number of choices will maximize your chances of having the target person or group accept a change proposal you favor; it allows a choice to be made, but only from alternatives that are acceptable to you. It is important for you to phrase your questions as if a given event *will* take place and the target person or group is to choose only how or when. If you are faced with a limited number of alternatives and asked to choose from them, most likely you will do so; only in rare instances will you question the initial assumptions or raise additional alternatives. Compare the approach of a change agent who asks, "Can we get together sometime to discuss ways of improving this situation?" to one who says, "I've arranged to have the conference room available on either

Monday or Friday afternoon to discuss how we can change this situation. Which do you prefer?"

Advance Obligation

The advantages and disadvantages of a commitment become prominent at different times. The advantages are more likely to be clear when the action will take place in the future. As the event becomes more immediate, however, the disadvantages become more eminent. Since most people feel compelled to meet their obligations, it is to your advantage to gain a commitment from them to participate in a change effort well in advance of its planned occurrence. If the target person or group feels that they have made a commitment, it will be difficult to renege when the anxieties associated with the approach of the event occur.

Positive Expectations

Telling the target person or group that you expect that they will be valuable participants in a change effort often acts as a self-fulfilling prophecy—i.e., they will fulfill your expectations in order to prove themselves worthy of your high regard. Using this approach also decreases the possibility of unwilling participation in your change effort because the target person or group will feel that they are important and are doing something valuable for you—which they will be.

Compliments

Attempting to change someone by using criticism will have negative consequences even if the strategy is successful. People usually regard criticism as "a slap in the face" and react defensively and with hostility toward its source. We are suggesting that you phrase your criticism in positive terms and frost it with preceding compliments. For example, a line manager says to a staff group leader, "We like your work very much. If your people would take a little more interest in personally relating these ideas with ours, we could probably make even better use of them," instead of, "Your people think they are such experts that they won't even come down off their high horse to relate to us as human beings, so that we can understand what they're talking about."

Indirect Comparisons

Another way of suggesting improvements without putting others on the defensive is to use indirect comparisons—that is, corrective information is given in reference to another person or group involved in a similar situation. It is important, of course, that the target person or group be aware that they are behaving in a similar fashion in order for this tactic to be effective. If the target person or group is aware of their behavior, indirect comparisons will allow them to evaluate the suggestions without losing face or becoming defensive.

Holding Out

Holding out, a blocking strategy, is a method of preventing a decision from being made or calling attention to a negative program, which needs your approval or participation to be successful. (Sometimes this is the only strategy a change agent, performing as a Catalyst, can muster.) Failing to cooperate or go along with a decision or plan of action is dangerous and unpleasant, but in some situations the risk you take and abuse you receive are necessary to get your point across.

Going Around Superiors

You may find yourself in a situation where your superiors in the organization simply will not agree to even consider a change which you feel is vitally necessary for the organization. Under such conditions, you may feel that your only alternative is to go over your superior's head to gain suport for the desired change. This is a dangerous maneuver as it violates your supervisor's trust and makes you vulnerable to any penalties he is able to apply. If you have applied the ten principles presented earlier in this chapter for being a successful inside change agent, and you still want to proceed, your chances of succeeding are fairly good. Because of the magnitude of the possible negative consequences associated with this strategy, however, we recommend that it only be used in desperate situations.

Threatening Resignation

This is *the* ultimate weapon. If you are considered a valuable employee, your opposition will listen to you when you lay your job on the line. Obviously, this is an extremely dangerous strategy. The warnings administered with respect to "going around superiors" should be doubled or tripled in this case. Never "call wolf" with this strategy. Don't use it unless you mean it. If your opposition senses that you are bluffing and calls you on it, you will lose face and perhaps even your job.

Media Dissemination

Disseminating your ideas and proposals to others in the organization through newspapers, memos, or bulletin announcements is a relatively risk-free strategy which may be effective in gaining the support of opinion leaders or other influential organizational members. This approach will raise the awareness of the target person or group concerning a problem situation and start them thinking of ways to improve it. The same thing can be done on a smaller scale by word of mouth.

Support Groups

Support groups, consisting of organizational members who share a common concern for changing some aspect of the organization, are important for testing ideas and expressing empathy; and they support one another under heavy opposition. Support group meetings produce increased awareness about the nature and consequences of a proposed change and provide us with a better perspective on how to gain more control over our organization life.

Gatekeeping

Gatekeeping refers to a Process-Helper role, where you facilitate the communication process so that everyone concerned has an equal chance to participate. Simple comments such as, "What do some of the rest of you think?" or "We haven't heard from Jim yet," may decrease the influence of some of your more assertive opponents and solicit important information from those who support you and the desired change.

ORGANIZATIONAL CHANGE STRATEGIES FOR MORE EXPERIENCED FACILITATORS

This section summarizes some of the more sophisticated organizational change strategies and indicates their potential application. It is suggestive of the multitude of options which do exist; it is not, however, a complete catalog of strategies. A guide for applying the strategies to the most appropriate level of intervention—individual, group, or total organization—is provided, as is a list of references which describe how to apply the strategies for maximum effectiveness and which contain many more strategy options. We recommend that before attempting to apply a particular strategy which appears to fit your situation you check the references to determine its specific process and intended effects; also make sure that you possess the facilitator skills and experience to make it successful.

As you read through the suggested references, you will develop an in-depth conceptual understanding of the theory and method behind each strategy. We suggest that, if you do not yet possess the skills or experience required for most of these strategy applications, you either link-up with an experienced outside consultant or complete one of the better-known change-agent training programs, such as those offered by the National Training Laboratories, Washington D.C., or University Associates, San Diego, California.

The summaries of change strategies which follow are listed in alphabetical order. You should refer to the Guide to Selecting Organization Change Strategies, which is given later in this chapter, to determine their recommended target application and suggested references.

1 *Authority analysis study.* This is a diagnostic method used to help administrators deal more effectively with the problems of delegation and control. It involves working with the administrator and those who report to him or her. The basic process consists of gathering data, discussing the data, and implement-

ing appropriate action plans. Objectivity, which can be often obtained by the noninvolvement of an outsider, is necessary in order for this type of study to be successfully implemented; otherwise, a considerable degree of resistance and distortion may be expected.

2 *Career planning.* Career planning helps individuals to develop a desirable and feasible career objective and to plan the steps necessary to attain it. It also involves development of short- and long-range work goals and professional objectives. Career planning is usually undertaken during periods of career decisions or changes. It frequently takes place in a group setting so that the group can give feedback on the reality of an individual's goals. Including higher-ranking officers in planning groups can provide reality checks. Also, the inclusion of Personal Development Strategies based on personal and organizational assessments are a good source to proceed from.

3 *Confrontation meeting.* This strategy is used for conflict resolution and sometimes for goal setting. Data are collected from the parties involved in a conflict situation regarding disagreements and then are fed back to the participants in a nonthreatening way. The objectives are for both sides to gain a better understanding of how the other perceives the situation, to clarify misunderstandings, and to formulate plans for improving the situation.

4 *Fish bowl.* This technique can be used to improve communication and collaboration between two interfacing groups or to improve the internal process of a single on-going group. If two groups are to be analyzed, one group meets to discuss its own problems and the problems it has with the other group; the other group sits around them in an outer circle, listening and observing. The groups then reverse positions and the process is repeated. If a group wants to analyze its processes, it divides into two groups and forms two concentric circles—an inner circle and an outer circle. The group in the inner circle discusses a problem; when it has finished, the group in the outer circle provides feedback on member roles and processes. The groups then exchange positions and the process is repeated.

5 *Force-field analysis.* This technique involves analyzing a situation, which a group, individual, or organization would like to change, by identifying the driving and the restraining forces that impinge on the situation. These forces can be identified by using data-gathering methods or through the process of group consensus. A unique aspect of this technique is that it concentrates on one significant problem. It also can be used at all levels.

6 *Group therapy within organizations.* The purpose of this technique is to stimulate change in the organization by means of group processes occurring at every level in the organization. The immediate goal is the improvement of organizational members' understanding of their interrelationships and personal motives; the remote goal being organizational restructuring by responsible organizational members. Trained therapists should be employed on a long-range basis in order for this technique to be effective.

7 *Managerial grid.* This is a systematic, long-range, organizational development process, which is made up of six phases:
   a Laboratory seminars for identifying and analyzing managerial behavior as it relates to people and production.
   b Team building.
   c Inter-group building and conflict resolution.
   d Development of strategic organizational development goals and plans.
   e Implementation of strategic organizational development goals and plans.
   f Critique, measurement, and recycling of any or all of the first five phases.

8 *Management by objectives* (MBO). MBO attempts to establish a better "fit" between personal and organizational goals by increasing communications and shared perceptions between the managers and their subordinates, either individually or as a group. The emphasis is on mutual understanding and performance with the objective of reducing role conflict and ambiguity. The steps in the MBO process are as follows:

a Joint work group/member definition of both overall and individual goals and tasks and the establishment of action plans for the achievement of both.
   b Joint manager/subordinate goal-setting.
   c Establishment of action plans for goals.
   d Establishment of success criteria.
   e Review and recycle.
   f Maintenance of records.
9 *Organizational mirror.* When the organizational-mirror technique is used, meetings are held in a "fish bowl" environment, where a subgroup collects feedback on its behavior from several key groups or organizations that are affected by its performance. A particular group may, for example, meet with interfacing units within its own organization as well as with suppliers or customers. Target results include lists of specific tasks for improving behavior along with a clearer understanding of important links and needs.
10 *Power-conflict study.* This is a diagnostic-intervention technique that is directed toward resolving intergroup-conflict problems and is appropriate when conflict between groups has become costly enough to warrant an effort to resolve the causes. This technique consists of two phases: (1) data are gathered from both groups regarding critical decision processes and the attitudes of each group; (2) a confrontation meeting is held to discuss the data which have been collected. A "neutral party, who should be competent in both data-gathering and group-discussion facilitation, conducts the power-conflict study.
11 *Process observation and feedback.* This technique is employed to analyze what takes place between members of groups as they work together or meet in sensitivity training sessions. A process observer, usually a facilitator who is not a member of the group, joins the group, but does not participate in the discussion. Feedback from the processor observer may be given immediately or reserved until the end of the session. This technique may be used as in change efforts or as a regular part of staff meetings.

12 *Role playing.* This technique assigns roles to participants, who are told the circumstances which led to the situation they are to enact. The participants become as involved as possible with their roles and react to other participants as if the situation were real. Roles are frequently rotated to increase empathy and to broaden each participant's perspective on problems and behaviors. Observers give feedback on the participants' reactions and analyze their behavior.

13 *Sensing.* This is a group-interviewing technique that is used for organizational diagnosis and to improve communication. Members of all levels and factions meet in an unstructured group-interview to discuss their concerns. These sessions are recorded and the information is passed on to higher-level administrators to get a "sense" of the organizational climate.

14 *Sensitivity training.* This strategy consists of an extended series of (more-or-less) unstructured group sessions which give the participants an opportunity to examine their group processes in the "here-and-now." These training group (T-group) sessions are intended to increase the participants' sensitivity to others and to the way others react to them. The participants learn how to establish norms of trust and openness to giving and receiving new ideas and feedback.

15 *Survey feedback.* This process involves the systematic collection of data from the members of an organization concerning matters such as job satisfaction, superiors' behavior, motivation, etc. The data are summarized and fed back to organizational members to assist them when they are confronted with actual perception and performance problems. This process helps the organization to "unfreeze" by revealing actual, but heretofore unspoken, conflicts and problems, thereby allowing a more accurate self-diagnosis so that specific remedial actions can be taken.

16 *Team building.* This technique contains a collection of related interventions for improving the effectiveness and satisfaction of people working together. The team-building technique is utilized by the manager and subordinates in a "work family," although it can also be successfully used with peer groups or

GUIDE TO SELECTION ORGANIZATION CHANGE STRATEGIES*

Strategy	Change target			References†
	Individual	Group	Organization	
Authority analysis study		X	X	Mahler
Career planning	X			Rush, Fordyce, Weil
Confrontation meeting			X	Bechard
Fish bowl	X	X	X	Fordyce, Weil
Force-field analysis	X	X		Lewin, Fordyce, Weil
Group therapy within organizations		X	X	Jaques
Managerial grid		X	X	Blake, Mouton
Management by objectives (MBO)		X		Odiorne
Organizational mirror		X	X	Fordyce, Weil
Power-conflict study		X		Mahler
Process observation/ feedback		X		Rush
Role-playing	X	X		Fordyce, Weil
Sensing			X	Fordyce, Weil
Sensitivity training	X	X		Schein, Bennis
Survey feedback		X	X	Mahler
Team building		X		Blake, Mouton, Rush
Transactional analysis	X	X		Harris

* This guide is designed to show a number of potential uses of various strategies.
† References follow.

ad-hoc groups. The process is similar to that which occurs in sensitivity training groups in that it stresses the development of interpersonal competence among the participants, while it also addresses "back-home" work-related issues.

17 *Transactional analysis.* Although this technique is most often used in group psychotherapy, it has recently been used in connection with organizations as a means of improving communications between employees who deal with customers, clients, or the public. It is just beginning to be used for intracompany purposes, such as for analyzing supervisor-subordinate relationships. Transactional analysis analyzes behaviors between people and categorizes them into three ego states—parent, adult, and child. Satisfactory behavioral transactions occur when one person responds to another with the corresponding ego-state behavior—for example, adult-adult. Problems arise when transactions become crossed—for example, adult-child or child-parent. The objectives of applying this technique are to increase individuals' understanding of why they behave as they do and to improve the effectiveness of communications between people.

REFERENCES TO ORGANIZATION CHANGE STRATEGIES

BECKHARD, R., "The Confrontation Meeting," *Harvard Business Review,* 45 (1967): 149–55.

BLAKE, R., and J. MOUTON, *The Managerial Grid,* Houston, Texas: Gulf Publishing Company (1964).

BYRD, R. E., *A Guide to Personal Risk Taking,* New York: Amacom (1974).

CULBERT, S. A., *The Organization Trap and How to Get Out of It,* New York: Basic Books, Inc. (1974).

FORDYCE, J., and R. WEIL, *Managing with People—A Manager's Handbook of Organization Development Methods,* Reading, Mass.: Addison-Wesley (1971).

HARRIS, T., *I'm OK—You're OK: A Practical Guide to Transactional Analysis,* New York: Harper & Row (1967).

HAVELOCK, R. G., *The Change Agent's Guide to Innovation in Education,* Englewood Cliffs, N.J.: Educational Technology Publications (1973).

HUSE, E., *Organization Development and Change*, New York: West Publishing Company (1975).

JAQUES, E., *The Changing Culture of a Factory*, London: Tavistock Institute (1951).

LANGER, E. J., C. S. DWECK, *Personal Politics: The Psychology of Making It*, Englewood Cliffs, N.J.: Prentice-Hall (1973).

LEWIN, K., *Field Theory in Social Science: Selected Theoretical Papers*, New York: Harper & Row (1951).

MAHLER, W., *Diagnostic Studies*, Reading, Mass.: Addison-Wesley (1974).

ODIORNE, G., *Management by Objectives*, New York: Pitman (1965).

RUSH, H., *Organization Development: A Reconnaissance*, New York: The Conference Board (1973).

SCHEIN, E., W. BENNIS, *Personal and Organizational Change through Group Methods*, New York: Wiley (1965).

IMPLEMENTING JOE BRENNON'S CHANGE PLAN

At this point, Joe Brennon has completed his personal and organizational assessments and his Personal Development Strategy. His low Match-Mismatch Index indicated that his best strategy was to resign and find another position where his personal values would better "fit" those of the organization. However, Joe's case was complicated by his personal situation which made it highly desirable that he stay in the city where he currently resides. Given this consideration, Joe decided on his second alternative—that is, change the organization.

Specific Goals for Change

Joe's primary goal was to be promoted to associate professor. He diagnosed the problem as a lack of "fit" between his values and those of the university faculty. Joe was hesitant to alter his values or behavior, thus his immediate subgoal was to change the values of key faculty members to be more congruent with his.

Consequently, Joe's specific goals were:

1 Change the behavior of faculty members in order to obtain a favorable vote and be promoted to associate professor.

2 Change the attitudes and values of faculty members so that freedom of appearance and style is accepted.

Operationalizing Goals

Breaking his objectives down into measurable and observable dimensions, Joe asked himself specifically *what* had to be done and by *whom, when* these objectives had to be accomplished, and *how* he would *know* if these actions were successful. Joe operationalized his goals in the following manner:

1 What needs to be accomplished?
   a Raise the awareness of faculty members so that they understand that the attitude of the business community has changed and it no longer insists on conservative images for faculty members, and that personal appearance does not necessarily correlate with competence.
   b The attitudes of the senior faculty members need to be changed so that they will be more open to and accepting of others, who are different in appearance.
   c Enhance the rapport between Joe and his faculty colleagues.
   d Obtain commitments from key faculty members in order to change their behavior so that they will vote in favor of Joe's promotion to associate professor.
2 Joe realized that it was primarily his responsibility to initiate these changes. He could count on support from colleagues within his department and help from friends in the business community. Recognized academics at other institutions who were respected by the faculty members might be another source of assistance.
3 Joe had to move fast if he hoped to accomplish the goals he had established. Although he still had two years remaining on his contract, his last chance for a reconsideration was at the end of the current academic year, only eight months away. Joe realized that the information gathering, relationship building, and attitude changing he hoped to accomplish would require a great deal of effort. He would have to begin immediately.

4 In order to determine whether his efforts were successful, Joe asked some trusted colleagues to obtain feedback from other department members regarding their image of Joe and whether their attitudes were changing in a favorable way. Joe decided that he would talk to some of these people himself in order to clarify issues and enhance his rapport with them.

Strategies and Subgoals

In deciding which strategies to use in his change effort, Joe reviewed the five considerations for choosing a change strategy. He had plenty of training and practice in applying all types of organizational change techniques and he was aware of the special characteristics of his organization. It was Joe's relationship with the organization, which was perhaps the trickiest consideration, especially when the time restraints were considered. Given these constraints, Joe proceeded to review the strategies listed in this chapter and decided that the feasible alternatives included both interpersonal strategies and some broader organizational change techniques. He selected the following interpersonal strategies:

1 Use *directed thinking* in all encounters with departmental members in order to enhance his rapport with his colleagues.

2 Use *disclaimers* to prove to the others that they, as well as Joe, will benefit from a favorable vote.

3 Use *inoculation* to help counter negative arguments, which Joe is sure will arise again.

4 *Obligate in advance* whenever he can to gain support so that he will be more certain of that person's vote when the decision regarding his promotion is made.

5 Use *compliments* and indicate *positive expectations* to generate feelings of high self-esteem in faculty members—feelings which will be reinforced if they voted in a positive way.

6 Use *indirect comparisons* to universities in which freedom of appearance is allowed, especially those universities where the faculty members are of high prestige.

7 Use *media dissemination* to alert supporters outside and inside the university of the problem situation and solicit their support.
8 Create and maintain a *support group* to bolster his efforts and morale and to keep his supporters encouraged and active for his cause.

The organizational change strategies which seemed appropriate included:

1 A *confrontation meeting* between Joe's supporters and antagonists to clarify misunderstandings and raise their awareness of how each side perceived the issue.
2 Using *survey feedback* within the organization and in conjunction with the outside groups in the business community and at other universities. Data gathered from these internal and external surveys could reveal additional insights, unspoken problems, and a better frame of reference, hopefully one more favorable to Joe's case.

Building in Reward Systems

Joe figured that there were several payoffs available to him which were inherent in the strategies he had selected to implement. If he received advanced obligations, his feelings of security would increase. The indirect comparisons to other universities and their "different-appearing" faculty members would provide him with a positive reference group. Also, his support group would provide him with direct encouragement and feelings of self-worth.

Joe knew that it was also important for his supporters and those he convinced to come over to his side to have payoffs. There were several rewards his program could provide for these people—for example, compliments and high expectations that would generate feelings of positive self-esteem; indirect comparisons with other prestigious universities which allowed freedom in appearance that would promote feelings of being more avant-garde if the department reversed its earlier decision. Finally, survey data from the business community would contribute to the feeling that the university was moving in a direction which promised future rewards and support.

Check Points

In order to obtain timely feedback about the progress of his change effort, Joe decided to set up several check points. He established a schedule and set deadlines for mailing surveys so that the results would be returned in time for a meaningful analysis and presentation. After checking with his support group, Joe set up a mutually-agreed-upon schedule for regular bi-weekly meetings. It was agreed that feedback regarding the latest assessment of current opinions would be provided at these meetings. Joe felt that obtaining advanced obligations would give him a check on his progress.

Joe realized that this change plan required a tremendous amount of time and effort. After assessing the alternatives, however, he knew that it was his best choice and that obtaining positive results would satisfy his professional objectives. Now, Joe knew "where he was at." He understood the circumstances and was committed to making a change effort which he thought would benefit everyone.

Chapter 11
Concluding Notes

This chapter represents the end of a guided journey. We began by describing the feelings of alienation, dissatisfaction, and unfulfillment that many if not all of us experience in our everyday world of work, play, and intimate relations. Since we spend so many of our waking hours as members of organizations—be they work, social, civic, or family—these organizations exert a considerable influence over how we feel, act, and think. In a sense, we are never "islands." We need the structures, rewards, and sanctions that organizations provide to give us a sense of having roots, direction, and support. Organizations also provide us with opportunities to confirm our belief that we are worthwhile people and to actualize our potentials as unique individuals.

It is our belief that human beings are constantly searching for meaning in their lives that will satisfy their humanness. This journey for meaning in life has been operationalized in this book in terms of the actualization of values. We have used the term "value" to mean "that which a person senses is important to him or her based on needs and level of development, spiritual and philosophical outlook, rights, and responsibilities as a member of an organization." The organization also has needs, developmental stages, and values.

The age-old problem for many individuals has been how to interface with organizations without losing too much of the sense of meaning, satisfaction and fulfillment the individuals previously felt they had. Unfortunately, many of us believe that individuals are usually involved in lose-win relationships with their organizations. Studs Terkel's (1974) interview with the majority of workers described in his book, *Working,* bears this out. We believe that almost anyone can analyze a situation, make decisions, and implement a course of action which will increase their feelings of satisfaction and fulfillment.

We have encouraged you to be your own change agent. We have provided you with a commonsense theory and a game plan for finding a meaningful sense of direction in your search for fulfillment. We have provided you with exercises to increase your self-awareness, your awareness of your organization, and with strategies and techniques which almost guarantee the desired outcomes. The rest is up to you!

We have pointed out your options and provided you with a simple but accurate means of assessment and time-tested strategies for change. We have encouraged your commitment to your goals with the systematic self-reinforcing stages of the Personal Development Strategy, which will guide you on your journey; but only you can complete it. This Strategy has helped others to achieve meaning and fulfillment in their lives. We hope you will let it help you. You *can* make it happen!

REFERENCES

BYRD, R., *A Guide to Personal Risk Taking,* New York: Amacon (1974).

CANNON, J. T., *Business Strategy and Policy,* New York: Harcourt, Brace, and World, pp. 523–538 (1968).

CARKHUFF, R. R., and T. FRIEL, *Art of Developing a Career,* Amherst, Mass.: Human Resources Development Press (1974).

CARKHUFF, R. R., *Art of Problem Solving,* Amherst, Mass.: Human Resources Development Press (1974).

CARKHUFF, R. R., *How to Help Yourself: Art of Program Development,* Amherst, Mass.: Human Resources Development Press (1974).

COOPER, K., *The New Aerobics,* New York: Bantam (1970).

CYERT, R. M., and J. G. MARCH, *A Behavioral Theory of the Firm,* Englewood Cliffs, N. J.: Prentice-Hall (1963).

ERIKSON, E., *Childhood and Society* (2nd Ed.), New York: W. W. Norton (1963).

FRANKL, V., *Psychotherapy and Existentialism: Selected Papers on Logotherapy*, New York: Simon and Schuster (1967).

GARDNER, J. W., "How to Prevent Organizational Dry Rot," *Harper's Magazine*, October 1967.

GIBSON, J. L., J. M. IVANCEVICH, and J. H. DONNELLY, *Organizations: Structure, Process, Behavior*, Dallas, Texas: Business Publications (1973).

GLASSER, W., *The Identity Society*, New York: Harper and Row (1972).

GLUECK, W. F., "An evaluation of stages of corporate development in business policy," paper presented to the *Midwest Academy of Management*, Kent, Ohio (1974).

GOODMAN, D., and M. MAULTSBY, *Emotional Well-Being Through Rational Behavior Training*, Springfield: Charles C. Thomas (1974).

GOULD, R., "The phases of adult life: A study in developmental psychology," *Am. J. of Psychiatry*, **129** (No. 5):521–531 (1972).

GOULD, R., "Adult life stages: Growth toward self-tolerance," *Psychology Today*, **8** (No. 9):74–81 (1975).

GRENIER, L. E., "Evolution and revolution as organizations grow," *Harvard Business Review*, pp. 36–46, July-August 1972.

HAIRE, M., *Modern Organization Theory*, New York: Wiley (1959).

HARRISON, R., "Understanding your organization's character," *Harvard Business Review*, pp. 119–128, May-June 1972.

HAVIGHURST, R., *Human Development in Education*, New York: Longmans, Green (1953).

JACOBSON, E., *Progressive Relaxation*, Chicago: University of Chicago Press (1938).

KATZ, D., and R. L. KAHN, *The Social Psychology of Organizations*, New York: Wiley (1966).

KAUFMAN, H., *The Limits of Organizational Change*, University, Alabama: University of Alabama Press (1971).

LEVINSON, D., "The normal crises of the middle years," *Symposium*, Hunter College, March 1973.

LIPPITT, G. L., and W. H. SCHMIDT, "Crises in a developing organization," *Harvard Business Review*, pp. 102–112, November-December 1967.

MASLOW, A., *Eupsychian Management: A Journal*, Homewood, Ill.: Irwin-Dorsey (1964).

MASLOW, A., *Toward a Psychology of Being*, New York: Van Nostrand (1968).

NEWMAN, W. H., and J. P. LOGAN, *Management of Expanding Enterprises*, New York: Columbia University Press (1955).

O'NEILL, N., and G. O'NEILL, *Shifting Gears*, New York: Avon (1974).

PARKINSON, C. N., *Parkinson's Law*, Boston: Houghton-Mifflin (1957).

PERLS, F., *Gestalt Therapy Verbatim*, Lafayette: Real People Press (1969).

SHEEHEY, G., *Passages: Predictable Crises of Adult Life*, New York: Dutton (1976).

SPERRY, L., *Developing Skills in Contact Counseling*, Reading, Mass.: Addison-Wesley (1975).

SPERRY, L., and L. HESS, *Contact Counseling: Communication Skills for People in Organizations*, Reading, Mass.: Addison-Wesley (1974).

STARBUCK, W., "Organizational growth and development," J. March (ed.), *Handbook of Organizations*, Chicago: Rand McNally, pp. 451–533 (1965).

STEVENS, J., *Awareness: Exploring, Experimenting, Experiencing*, Moab: Real People Press (1971).

TERKEL, S., *Working*, New York: Pantheon (1974).

TOFFLER, ALVIN, *Future Shock*, New York: Random House (1970).

YUCHTMAN, E., and S. E. SEASHORE, "A system resource approach to organizational effectiveness," *Am. Sociological Rev.*, **32**, pp. 891–902, December 1967.

Index

Adler, A., 30
Adult development,
  stages of, 17–25
  tasks, 25
Assessment,
  organization, 103
  personal, 78–79

Bonner, H., 73
Byrd, R., 139, 145, 186

Campbell, D., 75
Carkhuff, R., 28, 55, 114, 132
Case studies, 1–6
Change agent,
  inside, 169
  tips on being successful, 172–175
Combs, A., 73
Commitment, 139, 142–144
Contact counseling, 66–67
Cooper, K., 149
Culbert, S., 186
Cyert, R., 41

Decision-making, 118
Defensive behavior, 83
Dweck, C., 186
Developmental task, 18

Erikson, E., 18

Frames of reference, 15–16, 63
Frankl, V., 74–75
Friel, T., 28, 55

Gardner, J., 45
Glasser, W., 27
Goodman, D., 159
Gould, R., 18–19

Harrison, R., 50, 61
Havelock, R., 169, 175, 181, 186
Havighurst, R., 18, 26
Hess, L., 30

Jacobson, E., 151

Langer, E., 186
Levinson, D., 18–19

March, J., 41
Maslow, A., 71, 73
Match-mismatch index, 117–118
Maultsby, M., 159
Maximization principle, 40
Menninger, K., 111

National Training Laboratory, 192

O'Neill, G., 77
O'Neill, N., 77
Options to a problem, 111–113
Organizations,
  assessment, 103
  barriers to change, 43–45
  climate, 50
  stages of growth, 45–49

Parkinson, N., 40
Performance criteria, 127
Perls, F., 143
Personal Development Strategy (PDS),
  definition, 8, 65–66
  steps, 9, 67–71

Personality styles,
  definition, 30
  types, 31–35
Program development steps, 132–134

Rogers, C., 73

Self-actualization,
  definition, 12, 71
  characteristics, 72, 127
Self-actualizing, 74
Sheehy, G., 19, 63
Shostrum, E., 72, 74, 75
Sperry, L., 30, 66
Stevens, J., 88
Synergy, 31

Terkel, S., 206
Toffler, A., 64

University Associates, 192

Values,
  definition, 26
  types, 27, 55, 56, 90